SHEPHERD'S NOTES

SHEPHERD'S NOTES

When you need a guide through the Scriptures

Revelation

BROADMAN
&HOLMAN
PUBLISHERS

Nashville, Tennessee

Shepherds Notes®—*Revelation*

© 1999 Broadman & Holman Publishers, Nashville, Tennessee

All rights reserved

Printed in the United States of America

ISBN# 0–8054–9017–5

Dewey Decimal Classification: 228.07

Subject Heading: BIBLE. N.T. REVELATION

Library of Congress Card Catalog Number: 98–48092

Library of Congress Cataloging-in-Publication Data

Blum, Edwin, 1935–

    Revelation / Edwin Blum, editor [i.e. author].

       p.   cm. — (Shepherd's notes)

    Includes bibliographical references.

    ISBN 0–8054–9017–5 (trade paper.)

       1. Bible.   N.T. Revelation—Study and teaching.   I. Title.

  II. Series

  BS2825.5B58 1999   98–48092

                                        CIP

1 2 3 4 5 6   03 02 01 00 99

CONTENTS

Dear Reader:

Shepherd's Notes are designed to give you a quick, step-by-step overview of every book of the Bible. They are not meant to be substitutes for the biblical text; rather, they are study guides intended to help you explore the wisdom of Scripture in personal or group study and to apply that wisdom successfully in your own life.

Shepherd's Notes guide you through the main themes of each book of the Bible and illuminate fascinating details through appropriate commentary and reference notes. Historical and cultural background information brings the Bible into sharper focus.

Six different icons, used throughout the series, call your attention to historical-cultural information, Old Testament and New Testament references, word pictures, unit summaries, and personal application for everyday life.

Whether you are a novice or a veteran at Bible study, I believe you will find *Shepherd's Notes* a resource that will take you to a new level in your mining and applying the riches of Scripture.

In Him,

David R. Shepherd
Editor-in-Chief

DESIGNED FOR THE BUSY USER

Shepherd's Notes for Revelation is designed to provide an easy-to-use tool for getting a quick handle on this Bible book's important features, and for gaining an understanding of its message. Information available in more difficult-to-use reference works has been incorporated into the *Shepherd's Notes* format. This brings you the benefits of many more advanced and expensive works packed into one small volume.

Shepherd's Notes are for laymen, pastors, teachers, small-group leaders and participants, as well as the classroom student. Enrich your personal study or quiet time. Shorten your class or small-group preparation time as you gain valuable insights into the truths of God's Word that you can pass along to your students or group members.

DESIGNED FOR QUICK ACCESS

Bible students with time constraints will especially appreciate the timesaving features built in the *Shepherd's Notes*. All features are intended to aid a quick and concise encounter with the heart of the message.

Concise Commentary. Short section summaries provide quick "snapshots" of of this pivotal letter.

Outlined Text. A comprehensive outline covers the entire text of Revelation. This is a valuable feature for following the narrative's flow, allowing for a quick, easy way to locate a particular passage.

Shepherd's Notes. These summary statements appear at the close of every key section of the narrative. While functioning in part as a quick summary, they also deliver the essence of the message presented in the sections which they cover.

Icons. Various icons in the margin highlight recurring themes in Revelation, aiding in selective searching or tracing of those themes.

Sidebars and Charts. These specially selected features provide additional background information to your study or preparation. These include definitions as well as cultural, historical, and biblical insights.

Maps. These are placed at appropriate places in the book to aid your understanding and study of a text or passage.

Questions to Guide Your Study. These thought-provoking questions and discussion starters are designed to encourage interaction with the truth and principles of God's Word.

DESIGNED TO WORK FOR YOU

Personal Study. Using the *Shepherd's Notes* with a passage of Scripture can enlighten your study and take it to a new level. At your fingertips is information that would require searching several volumes to find. In addition, many points of application occur throughout the volume, contributing to personal growth.

Teaching. Outlines frame the text of Revelation, providing a logical presentation of the message. Capsule thoughts designated as "Shepherd's Notes" provide summary statements for presenting the essence of key points and events. Personal Application icons point out personal application of John's message in Revelation, and Historical Context icons indicate where background information is supplied.

Group Study. *Shepherd's Notes* can be an excellent companion volume to use for gaining a quick but accurate understanding of the message of a Bible book. Each group member can benefit by having his or her own copy. The *Note's* format accommodates the study of or the tracing of the themes throughout Revelation. Leaders may use its flexible features to prepare for group sessions or use them during group sessions. Questions to guide your study can spark discussion of the key points and truths of Revelation.

LIST OF MARGIN ICONS USED IN REVELATION

 Shepherd's Notes. Placed at the end of each section, a capsule statement provides the reader with the essence of the message of that section.

 Old Testament Reference. Used when the writer refers to Old Testament Scripture passages that are related or have a bearing on the passage's understanding or interpretation.

 New Testament Reference. Used when the writer refers to New Testament passages that are related to or have a bearing on the passage's understanding or interpretation.

 Historical Background. To indicate historical, cultural, geographical, or biographical information that sheds light on the understanding or interpretation of a passage.

 Personal Application. Used when the text provides a personal or universal application of truth.

 Word Picture. Indicates that the meaning of a specific word or phrase is illustrated so as to shed light on it

INTRODUCTION

WHAT KIND OF BOOK IS THIS?

The book of Revelation is a unique book. There is nothing like it in the rest of the New Testament or in the Old Testament. It is a letter (like Paul's Epistles) sent to seven historical churches. It identifies itself as a prophecy (1:3; 19:10; 22:7). It has numerous symbols and features like Jewish apocalyptic writings. So it is an apocalyptic-prophetic letter or an apocalyptic prophecy in the form of a circular letter.

Revelation is a book that is full of allusions and references to the Old Testament, but it has hardly any full quotations like many New Testament books. The title for this book in the first line is *The Revelation of Jesus Christ*. The revelation is *of* Jesus Christ in two ways. First, He is the revealer (cp. Matt. 11:27; John 1:18), and second, He is the content or object of the revelation. We learn about the nature and activities of Jesus of Nazareth as He is today and His future victory or reign in this world.

Revelation is a fitting conclusion to the whole Bible. So as the Bible is read, themes in early books like Genesis and Exodus come to completion. The biblical narrative comes to its goals. The kingdom of God is established, sinful rebellion in the world and in heaven is punished, and humanity is redeemed and restored to personal fellowship with God.

WHAT IS REVELATION ABOUT?

Revelation describes a great conflict which began with a rebellion among the angels in heaven itself (cp. 12:7–8). This war between the forces of light and the forces of darkness

Apocalyptic describes writings that employ symbolic language to tell of a divine intervention which will take place in the future.

Revelation means "unveiling" or making known what was previously hidden.

Revelation promises to bless the person who reads it and applies it to his or her life (1:3; 22:7).

spread to earth and has continued from the time of Genesis 3 until today. Revelation describes the intensification and the culmination of the struggle in the climax of the ages. This warfare is between two kingdoms and two cities: God's kingdom versus Satan's kingdom (including rebellious humans); Babylon the great versus the New Jerusalem. Elements of this conflict include martyrs, persecutions, battles, and great judgments (cp. 1:9; 2:10; 2:13; 3:10; 6:9–11; 7:14; 11:7; 12:4, 6–7, 13; 17:14; 19:19; 20:7–8).

At face value, a good part of the book (chaps. 4–19) describes what it calls "the great tribulation" (7:14) or "the hour of trial" (3:10). This is a unique period in the history of the world which Jesus Himself predicted would be "days of distress" unequaled in the long time from creation (cp. Mark 13:14–19). This is a period of the reign of the Antichrist and also a time of great judgments on the earth. The following passages of Scripture are related to this "great tribulation" (Dan. 12:1; Joel 2:31; Jer. 30:7–8; Matt. 24:15–24; 2 Thess. 2:3–12; Rev. 13:8).

The major themes of this book are related to two symbols: "the lamb," used twenty-nine times, and "the throne," which occurs forty times. The *Lamb* is a title of Jesus and the *throne* is a symbol of God's rule and authority. The book describes the triumph of Jesus as God's Messiah and unique Son and how the sovereignty of God is manifested in redemption, judgment, rule, and the new creation.

WHO WROTE REVELATION?

The writer identifies himself as "John" (1:1, 4, 9; 22:8) and his writing as a prophecy (22:19). The book was accepted as Scripture and the author was understood to be John the apostle, who wrote three epistles and a Gospel.

However, beginning with Dionysius of Alexandria (died around 264), many have been opposed to the millennial (Rev. 20:1–7) teaching of the book, and arguments have developed against the authorship by John, son of Zebedee. Many modern scholars reject Johannine authorship, and there has been a neglect of this writing among the theologians. For example, Luther and Zwingli, early reformers, had little respect for the book. Calvin ignored it and wrote commentaries on the rest of the New Testament, and on a large part of the Old Testament. Part of the problem has been the use of the book by unorthodox teachers or by fanatics. Part of the neglect is due to its symbolism. Another part is its Jewishness or its millennial teaching which is contrary to the European church tradition since Augustine (died A.D. 430).

A good defense of Johannine authorship can be made. The early witness of the six church fathers named above could hardly be better. The following list shows some of the links between John's Gospel, his epistles, and the Revelation.

1. All books use simple, common Greek vocabulary.
2. In the Gospel and Revelation, there is a similar use of *logos*.
3. In the Gospel and Revelation, there is a similar use of *sign* and *signify*.
4. In the Gospel and Revelation, common key terms are *witness* and *testify*.
5. Common use of the verb (*nikao*) to conquer, or *overcome*.
6. Both the Gospel (6:31) and Revelation (2:17) use a *manna* theme.

The Greek word *alethinos* (true, truth) occurs twenty-eight times in the New Testament. Of these, it occurs in John's Gospel nine times, John's epistles four times, and Revelation ten times—or twenty three of the twenty-eight usages in the New Testament. Other similarities can be found with the use of a concordance to compare the usage of words and phrases.

7. Both the Gospel (4:21) and Revelation (21:22) say that a temple is not needed for worship.

8. Both the Gospel (10:1) and Revelation (7:17) say Jesus is the Shepherd.

9. Both the Gospel (4:10, 14; 7:38) and Revelation (7:17; 21:6; 22:17) use the terms *water* and *springs* to describe salvation or eternal life.

10. Both the Gospel (19:37) and Revelation (1:7) have a unique citation from Zechariah 12:10. Neither book cites the Scripture often.

11. The structures of both the Gospel and Revelation are built on *sevens*: seven signs, seven churches, and so forth.

12. Common usage in John's Gospel, his epistles, and Revelation of the expression "keep the commandments."

13. Common dualism in all John's writings: God/Satan; world/church; good/evil; light/darkness.

While it cannot be absolutely proven that John son of Zebedee wrote the Revelation, the weight of evidence is heavy in favor of this conclusion.

WHEN WAS IT WRITTEN?

From Irenaeus in A.D. 180 (John saw the revelation at the close of Domitian's reign), the majority view has been that the date is A.D. 95. This fits with internal and external evidence.

AUTHOR AND AUDIENCE

According to Revelation, John was exiled to the prison island of Patmos during the reign of the Roman emperor Domitian because of his commitment to Jesus Christ and His Word (1:9). John, who was one of the "inner circle" of Jesus' disciples (Peter, James, and John), ministered first in the Jerusalem church but later moved to

Ephesus. John's later ministry during the reign of Domitian (A.D. 81–96) ran into conflict with the Roman government. Since the time of Nero (A.D. 64), Christians were viewed as "enemies of mankind" who practiced an illegal religion.

The audience for Revelation was seven literal churches in Roman Asia. But the whole letter was sent to each one and applied to all Christians (1:4, 11; 2:1, 8, 18, etc.). For the universal application, see 1:3; 2:7, 11, 17, 29; 22:6–7, 9, 16, 18–19. As a book of the Bible, it is God's Word not only to the churches of the first century but also to the churches of all ages.

Ephesus was a leading church in the Roman province of Asia. Under Paul, Ephesus became a center for evangelism and teaching (Acts 19:9–10).

STRUCTURE AND OUTLINE

Prologue	1:1–8
John's Commission and Vision of Jesus	1:9–20
The Letters to the Seven Churches	Chapters 2–3
The Vision of the Heavenly Throne Room	Chapters 4–5
The Seven Seal Judgments	6:1–8:5
The Sealing of the 144,000	7:1–17
The Great Multitude in White Robes	8:1–5
The Seven Trumpet Judgments	8:6–11:19
The Angel with the Little Scroll	10:1–11:13
The Two Witnesses	11:14–19
The Cosmic and Earthly Struggles	Chapters 12–14
The Beast out of the Sea	Chapters 13:1–10
The Beast out of the Land	13:11–18
The Seven Bowl Judgments	Chapters 15–16
Babylon the Great Doomed	17:1–19:10
The Return of the Lord	19:11–21
The Thousand-Year Reign of Christ	20:1–6
The Final Judgments	20:7–15
The New Heaven and New Earth	21:1–22:5
The New Jerusalem	
Epilogue	22:6–21

HOW SHOULD REVELATION BE INTERPRETED?

Because this book is unique, it has been interpreted in many ways down through the centuries. The following synopsis will outline the major options which are not entirely in opposition to one another:

1. *Poetic-symbolic view.* The book is understood as a dramatic poem of the triumph of God. The poem is more like an abstract or expressionist painting than a blueprint for the ages. Others do not call it a poem but emphasize spiritual interpretation.

2. *Historical-critical view.* This view does not usually hold to prophecy as a genuine gift which is able to "see" the future. The events of the book are understood in terms of the first-century Roman Empire and the fall of Jerusalem (A.D. 70).

3. *Historicist view.* This approach sees the course of church history revealed in the visions.

4. *The futurist, or eschatological view.* This view holds that the main thrust of the book concerns the future. The events from chapter 4 to the end are mainly but not exclusively about events of the great tribulation, the return of Jesus Christ, the thousand-year reign, the last judgment, and the eternal state.

This *Shepherd's Notes'* interpretation will be futurist while utilizing insights from the other points of view. As indicated in the section entitled *What Is This Book About?* a normal reading of the text puts a large part (chaps. 4–19) into the future tribulation. While using many symbols, John did intend that his readers would be able to grasp the meaning and understand what was coming in the future.

The use of an interpreting angel is common in what is called apocalyptic literature, and this sometimes is found in the Old Testament prophetic books, especially in Zechariah (1:9, 12, 14; 2:3; 3:6; 4:1, 11).

In the ancient world, not everyone could read (some estimate only 20–30 percent were able) and not many could afford books.

PROLOGUE (1:1–8)

Introduction to the Book (1:1–3)

John explains what this writing is about. It is an *apokalypsis* or "unveiling" of Jesus Christ which God gave to him. The Father and the Son are united in revealing the nature and future of Jesus (cp. Matt. 11:25–27; John 5:19, 8:26). Jesus sends an angel to help John in the understanding of the visions. John is given this revelation so he can transmit it for the church's profit.

Revelation 1:3 indicates that the oral reading of this book would be done in the Christian congregations (cp. Col. 4:16; 1 Thess. 5:27). A blessing is pronounced upon everyone who responds positively to the message. This blessing is the first of seven in the book (1:3; 14:13; 16:15; 19:9; 20:6; 22:7; 22:14), and all seven point out what is of special importance.

The Seven Blessings

BLESSED ARE THOSE:	[REF.]
Who hear and obey	(1:3)
Who die in the Lord	(14:13)
Who look for Christ's return	(16:15)
Who are invited to the messianic banquet	(19:9)
Who have part in the first resurrection	(20:6)
Who keep the words of the prophecy of this book	(22:7)
Who wash their robes (cp. 7:14)	(22:14)

John says that "the time is near" (v. 3). From John the Baptist, from Jesus, and from the apostles, there is a constant emphasis on the time of crisis or decision. In the book of Revelation the following passages announce the nearness of the end (1:1, 3; 2:16, 25; 3:11, 20; 6:11; 10:6; 11:2–3; 12:6, 12; 17:10; 22:6–7, 10, 12, 20).

The Address, Greeting, and Ascription (1:4–6)

John addresses his prophecy to the seven churches in Roman proconsular Asia (this today is western Turkey). These churches were chosen because of John's knowledge of them and ministry among them. These churches are representative of all churches at that time and of churches today. So the message has individual and local significance as well as universal application.

The message comes from both the Father and the Son. The "seven spirits" cannot be exactly identified (cp. Isa. 11:2; Rev. 4:5; 5:6). The Son is depicted in a number of titles which show His nature and work. Christians are a kingdom of priests (cp. Exod. 19:6) who have direct access to God and minister to Him in worship and minister to a world in darkness.

The Theme (1:7–8)

The theme of the book is the return of Jesus the Messiah in the Second Coming. He is the same person who came to Bethlehem as a baby and went to the cross as the Suffering Servant of Isaiah 53. But in His return, He comes as the victorious "Son of man" who will judge the earth in righteousness and inaugurate God's rule as the kingdom of God on earth. Verse 7 combines elements from two key Old Testament prophecies: Daniel 7:13, which describes the coming reign

Christians of today should remember that Jesus told His disciples to watch and wait and that no one knows the exact time of His return except the Father in heaven (Mark 13:32–33).

The Seven Spirits

The NIV uses "sevenfold Spirit" as an alternative reading. This is another way of saying *the Holy Spirit*.

Patmos was a small island (ten miles by six miles) in the Aegean Sea located about thirty-seven miles southwest of Miletus. The Romans used such places for political exiles. John's mention of the island in Revelation 1:9 probably means that he was such a prisoner, having been sent there for preaching the gospel. Eusebius (an early church father) wrote that John was sent to Patmos by Emperor Domitian in A.D. 95 and released after one and one-half years.

The vision which preceded John's writing is similar to Isaiah's (6:1) and Ezekiel's (chap. 1).

The purpose of Christians and churches is to show God and Jesus to the world.

of the Son of Man, and Zechariah 12:10, which predicts the piercing of the Messiah (John 19:37). All the "peoples of the earth" (not just of Israel) will have regret and remorse when the regal nature of Jesus is revealed in its divine splendor.

THE CIRCUMSTANCES OF THE COMMISSION (1:9–11)

John was in exile on a prison island called Patmos. Most likely, around A.D. 95, the Roman government began some scattered persecution of Christians. Nero had already done this in Rome in A.D. 64 and soon after, both Peter and Paul were killed. John's ministry had focused on Jesus and His Word. Rome was beginning to exalt the emperor as a semidivine being and the Christian faith was illegal.

John's commission came in a dramatic way while he was worshiping on a Sunday. A trumpet voice summoned him to write a scroll and send it to the seven churches.

THE REVELATION OF THE GLORIFIED JESUS (1:12–16)

John first saw seven golden lampstands and someone like a "son of man." The lampstand (cp. Exod. 25:31–37) is a symbol of the church (according to 1:20), and its function is to bring light to a darkened world (cp. Matt. 5:14–16). "Son of Man" was a favorite self-designation of Jesus. It had a number of Old Testament connections. Jesus on earth was the suffering Son of Man, but now He is seen as a heavenly high priest with holiness and power. Just as we cannot look directly at the midday sun, so John could not look directly at His glory (cp. the similar experience John had at the transfiguration—Matt. 17:5–8).

JOHN'S RESPONSE AND JESUS' REASSURANCE (1:17–20)

Paul says that God dwells in unapproachable light (1 Tim. 6:15–16), and the ancient Israelites trembled before Mount Sinai as it blazed with divine fire. But Jesus touched John and reassured him that He had come to commission John to a special prophetic task. Verse 19 is often understood as an inspired three-point outline of the contents of the book: "what you have seen" (glorified Christ), "what is now" (the churches), and "what will take place later" (the Tribulation, millennium, judgment, and consummation). Others see a commission to write what he has seen—both what is and what is to follow (a two-point division). The three-point view seems better since John had only seen the risen Lord and not the churches or coming events at this time.

A major interpretive problem revolves around the "stars," which are interpreted as the "angels" of the churches. Four views are common: (1) A guardian angel for each church. Pro: "star" is interpreted by Christ as "angel." The normal meaning of "angel" in Revelation is a spirit being. Con: How do you write to an angel? (2) "Angel" = pastor, elder, or bishop. This is possible but unusual language. (3) "Angel" = messenger. The Greek word is sometimes used for this (Mal. 2:7; 3:1; Luke 9:52) and fits historical context. Roman postal service was for imperial use. Businesses and congregations had to develop their own mail system. (4) "Angel" = the church personified. This view seems best.

When only a little of God's glory shows, it is common to fall on one's face. "Like the appearance of a rainbow in the clouds on a rainy day, so was the radiance around him. This was the appearance of the likeness of the glory of the LORD. When I saw it, I fell facedown, and I heard the voice of one speaking" (Ezek. 1:28). "As he came near the place where I was standing, I was terrified and fell prostrate. 'Son of man,' he said to me, 'understand that the vision concerns the time of the end'" (Dan. 8:17; see also Isa. 6 and Josh. 5:14).

■ *Jesus, the resurrected Lord, appeared to John*
■ *in a vision and commissioned him to write to*
■ *seven churches in the Roman province of*
■ *Asia. The content of his writing is to be a*
■ *series of visions of the future and of the*
■ *present.*

QUESTIONS TO GUIDE YOUR STUDY

1. What are the seven blessings promised in Revelation?
2. Where was John when he saw the vision recorded in Revelation?
3. What was John's response to Jesus' appearance?

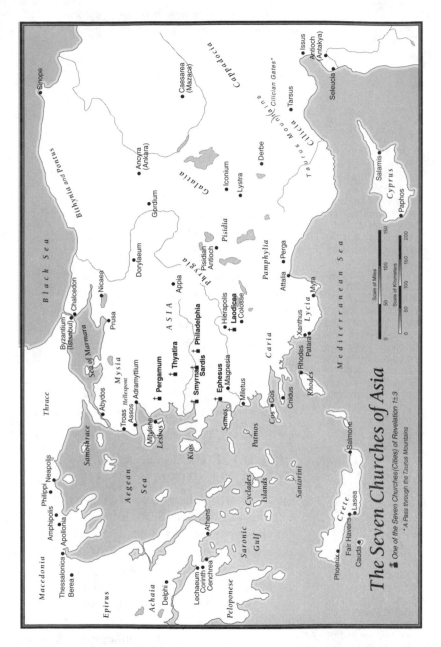

Taken from *Holman Book of Biblical Charts, Maps, and Reconstructions* (Nashville, Tenn.: Broadman & Holman Publishers, 1993), p. 133.

THE LETTER TO EPHESUS: THE LOVELESS CHURCH (2:1–6)

Each letter follows a similar pattern, but not all elements occur in each:

"And the LORD God said, 'The man has now become like one of us, knowing good and evil. He must not be allowed to reach out his hand and take also from the tree of life and eat, and live forever.' So the LORD God banished him from the Garden of Eden to work the ground from which he had been taken. After he drove the man out, he placed on the east side of the Garden of Eden cherubim and a flaming sword flashing back and forth to guard the way to the tree of life" (Gen. 3:22–24).

- command to write,
- description of the glorified Lord,
- positive evaluation,
- encouragement, warning,
- exhortation to the spiritually alert, and
- promise to the overcomer.

Jesus is in the midst of the churches and He knows what is going on. The church in Ephesus was battle-tested and orthodox, but somehow it had lost its love. Love is primary. Without it the church has no reason to exist. The exhortation is to all the churches and so is the promise. The tree of life (Gen. 2:9; 3:22–24) lost in Eden is regained in paradise (Rev. 22:2). The dying thief on the cross was promised this by Jesus (Luke 23:43).

THE LETTER TO SMYRNA: THE PERSECUTED CHURCH (2:7–11)

The word *Smyrna* is connected to myrrh and to suffering in the Bible. Some people and some churches are called to suffer. Today in eighty countries in the world (of 180 in the U.N.), there is persecution of Christians. Jesus reveals Himself as sovereign over death. He calls His people to be faithful to Him in spite of economic or political persecution which may lead to death. The Christian is the winner in the race of life and receives a wreath or garland which is a picture of eternal life (cp. 1 Cor. 9:25; 2 Tim. 4:8; James 1:2; 1 Pet. 5:4).

"On each side of the river stood the tree of life, bearing twelve crops of fruit, yielding its fruit every month. And the leaves of the tree are for the healing of the nations" (Rev. 22:2).

THE LETTER TO PERGAMUM: THE COMPROMISING CHURCH (2:12–17)

This church was located in the first city in Asia Minor that was the official center for emperor worship. The city was also a center for the worship of Askepios Soter and Zeus Soter. Both were connected to the serpent image. The expression "where Satan sits enthroned" may refer to a large throne altar on top of a high granite citadel. One of the major issues of first-century Christianity was separation or accommodation to paganism. Much of the business life was connected to trade guilds or organizations which met for meals that were held in temple halls. The meat sacrificed to these idols was served at their banquets. Often sexual immorality was a part of these banquets. From Balaam (about 1400 B.C.; cp. Num. 22:1–24 and 25:1–3), who corrupted Israel, to the Nicolaitans of John's days, God's people have been tempted to make accommodations to pagan culture and its destructive practices. Paul wrote often of this issue (1 Cor. 8:1–12; 10:14–33).

To those who compromise, Jesus warned of His coming judgment. To those who resist, He promised "hidden manna" and a "white stone." Manna was the food God's people lived on in the wilderness wanderings (Exod. 16:32–34). Jesus is the real manna for Christians to live on (John 6:48–51). The "white stone" means acceptance by God (compare our idiom "black-balled"). On the stone is a new name. Jesus changed the name of Cephas to *Peter* and often in the Old Testament, God changed the names of His people as He gave them spiritual blessings (cp. *Jacob = Heel-Grabber* to *Israel = Prince of God* or *He Who Struggles with God*; Gen. 32:28).

Today, Christians in business must be wary of compromise at trade conventions, drinking parties, and other similar occasions. Often in the business world, people are corrupted by gambling, immorality, alcohol, and drugs. In some cultures, these are tools for business advantage over the weak.

THE LETTER TO THYATIRA: THE CORRUPT CHURCH (2:18–29)

This letter addresses a church which compromised with paganism. However, this church seems more corrupt. The city was prominent for its trade guilds. Christian workers were at the mercy of organized pagan society. A woman claiming to be a prophetess arose. She encouraged accommodation to pagan culture. Her promotion of paganism was like that of Jezebel in the Old Testament (1 Kings 16:29; 2 Kings 9:30).

The decision of the first major church meeting (recorded in Acts 15) spoke to sexual immorality and meats offered to idols.

Jesus reveals Himself to this church as One who disciplines His people. Physical death was the penalty for some sins in the early church as God taught about His holiness (cp. Acts 5:1–11; 1 Cor. 11:27–30).

Jesus rewards the overcomer with a gift of Himself in a new and special way—"the morning star" (cp. 22:16; Num. 24:17). The believer will share in the messianic rule of Jesus over the pagan nations of the world (Ps. 2:8–9). But a compromise now will lead to judgment. Resist the world now and rule with Christ in the millennium.

THE LETTER TO SARDIS: THE DEAD CHURCH (3:1–6)

"Pride goes before a fall." This proud city had been the capital of an empire and the home of the famous king Croesus. Twice in its history, secure in a high acropolis, the city failed to watch its defenses. An enemy army came, and by stealth, took the city. Jesus warns the sleeping church of His coming. "Christians—wake up!" "Be spiritually alert!" "Are you prepared for His coming?"

The faithful Christian will participate in the victory triumph of Jesus. The white garment was worn in Roman triumphs. We receive a white garment from Jesus symbolizing our righteousness. Our names are enrolled—not in a state citizen-register or a synagogue roll or even a royal archive, but in God's book of life (cp. Exod. 32:32–33). Jesus will bring our names before God the Father. He owns us as His friends and His brothers and calls each of us by name (John 15:13–14; Heb. 2:11–13; 1 John 3:1).

THE LETTER TO PHILADELPHIA: THE FAITHFUL CHURCH (3:7–13)

Jesus is in control of our lives. He is the Holy One (Isa. 40:25; John 6:69) who has the key of David (Isa. 22:22). This "key" is to the messianic kingdom. He rules over it and has brought us into it (Col. 1:13) to reign with Him (Rev. 20:4, 6). Christ gives spiritual opportunities to His people (cp. 1 Cor. 16:9) and to churches. When God opens a door, no power can resist. As Jesus promised Peter, not even Hades can resist (Matt. 16:18–19).

We live in a day of great spiritual opportunity. The churches in America and in many other countries have a "door flung wide open" by God. Missions, radio, TV, the Internet, movies, tapes, CDs, books, magazines, the Bible in English as a global language, little government interference—all combine to offer amazing outreach for the church.

Jesus warns of a time of trial for the whole pagan world. It is called the "great tribulation" or "the hour of trial" (Rev. 3:10; cp. Mark 13:19; Jesus calls it a uniquely horrible period of human history). This "testing" is upon the unbelieving inhabitants of the earth (3:10; 6:10; 8:13; 11:10; 13:8, 12, 14; 17:2, 8). Although many people will be saved during these years—7:14 says a "great multitude" (cp. 7:9)—the day is a day of great wrath and judgment on human sin and rebellion (Rev. 6:17).

The faithful church is preserved and protected and the individual is inscribed with God's name. This denotes permanent ownership. We are also promised to be a "pillar" in God's temple—an essential part with permanence.

THE LETTER TO LAODICEA: THE LUKEWARM CHURCH (3:14–22)

The description of Jesus in verse 14—"the Amen," "the Witness," the "Faithful and True"—have strong connections to the Gospel of John as major themes in that book. The phrase "the beginning of the creation of God" (NASB) means Jesus Christ is the Source of all creation (cp. John 1:1–3)—not that He is a part of the creation.

The city of Laodicea had problems with its water supply. Unlike the nearby cities of Colosse with good cold water or Hierapolis with hot water for thermal baths, Laodicea had only lukewarm water which made a person vomit!

Unfortunately, a church is often like its environment. This city was very rich, and this apparently led to complacency. How many "rich" Americans today are thankful enough to say "thanks" at their beautiful and bountiful meals? After a great earthquake in A.D. 60, the city of

Laodicea declared, "I don't need any help from the government to rebuild—I'm rich." The church can become complacent and lukewarm and fail to recognize its need of the Lord and His grace. This church was spiritually blind to its true condition.

Paul reminded the Corinthian church: "What do you have that you did not receive?" (1 Cor. 4:7). All comes from God; therefore, we must constantly go to Him. Jesus reveals Himself to this church as One who stands at the door and knocks. Perhaps this alludes to a monumental triple gate at the entrance to the city. But in the spiritual realm, Jesus is before each individual and graciously inviting each one to personal fellowship with Him (3:20).

Although each letter is addressed to a specific local church with its own unique problems, each letter has individual and universal applications to every Christian in every age. Jesus, the Lord, is in the center of our local churches, and He knows what each one is doing. For the church to prosper, it needs to follow the orders of the Lord.

QUESTIONS TO GUIDE YOUR STUDY

1. Which of these seven churches is most like your local church?
2. Summarize briefly Jesus' appraisal of each church.
3. What is the greatest danger to your church today?

How many other biblical people have been taken to heaven? (Gen. 5:24; Heb. 11:5; 2 Kings 2:11; Ps. 73:24; 2 Cor. 12:2; Phil. 1:23; 1 Thess. 4:17). What is your future destiny?

Worship

The most common Greek word is *prosky-neo* which means to "fall down before" or to prostrate oneself. In addition to the physical posture, the inner attitude of true worship is reverence, humility, and adoration.

Angel

The Hebrew and Greek words (*malack,* and *aggelos*) are not as specific as our English word. They mean "messenger" and describe the function of angels.

THE THRONE ROOM IN HEAVEN (4:1–6)

Just as "mission control" is the place that directs space exploration, the throne room in heaven controls the universe and, specifically, the action about to take place on earth. John was taken to heaven to see a vision of the future (4:1). What does God look like? John did not say other than His appearance was blazing like diamond and topaz (cp. 1 Tim. 6:16).

THE WORSHIP OF HEAVEN (4:6b–11)

Because we do not see God as He is in His glory and power, we do not worship Him as we should. Other created beings—the living creatures and the twenty-four elders—have a clearer vision so they can teach us. Both groups are most likely heavenly creatures of different classes of angels. We are not alone in the universe (cp. 2 Kings 6:16–17; Matt. 26:53; Heb. 12:22), but we share it with many other intelligent beings. Paul says other intelligent heavenly creatures are learning about God's wisdom through God's plan of salvation in the church (Eph. 3:10).

Since the worship of God is the center of the spiritual universe, should it not be the center of our lives? John saw the throne of God where the control of the universe takes place.

QUESTIONS TO GUIDE YOUR STUDY

1. How do biblical angels differ from the popular image of angels in today's culture?

2. Why should people worship the Lord?

3. What makes a person into a true worshiper (John 4:23)?

THE LAMB TAKES THE SCROLL OF DESTINY (5:1–5)

Only the Lamb of God who is also the Lion from Judah's tribe (Gen. 49:9–10) has the moral right to open the scroll which will reveal and bring about history's completion. The lion and the lamb represent two aspects of Jesus' nature: the royal and the sacrificial.

THE WORSHIP OF THE LAMB AND OF GOD THE FATHER (5:6–14)

A possible background for this chapter is in Deuteronomy 17:18–20 and 2 Kings 11:12 where a king took his position to rule. At the enthronement ceremony a covenant book was in his hand to guide him in his rule.

The fact that Jesus is to be worshiped shows that He is God. Yet He is not identical with the Father. But this doesn't mean that Christians have two or three Gods (Father, Son, and Spirit). The solution to this problem is the doctrine of the Trinity—three eternal persons within one Godhead or divine essence. The Athanasian Creed states: "We worship one God in Trinity, and Trinity in Unity; neither confounding the Persons, nor dividing the Substance."

When God delivered Israel out of Egypt, His people sang a song (Exod. 15). Because Jesus has won the victory over Satan, sin, and death, the whole heaven explodes into praise of the Lamb. The four living creatures, the twenty-four elders, the prayers of God's people, and myriads of angels combine in universal adoration: "You have made them to be a

The background for this vision is Ezekiel's book of woe (Ezek. 2; see also Ps. 139:16; Deut. 17:18–20; 2 Kings 11:12). This book is in the form of a scroll with seals. As each seal is opened, more of the scroll can be unfolded (cp. Dan. 12:4).

The Old Testament background of this scene is Daniel 7:10. Ten thousand times ten thousand ministered to God and the "Son of Man" was invested with the kingdom.

kingdom and priests to serve our God, and they will reign on the earth" (5:10).

Christians are now serving as Israel did (Exod. 19:6) with the tasks of worshiping God and making Him known to the world. The future is to share Christ's rule on earth (cp. Matt. 5:5; Rom. 8:17; Rev. 20:4). Jesus, as the One who died and is now victorious, holds the book of destiny for the world. By our union with Him, we have confidence as we face our future.

Singing to the Lord is a vital part of our Christian life. Redemption will lead to worship. Paul told Christians to "speak to one another with psalms, hymns and spiritual songs. Sing and make music in your heart to the Lord" (Eph. 5:19). How much do you sing?

QUESTIONS TO GUIDE YOUR STUDY

1. What do angels do?
2. What does it mean for evangelism that the Lamb has purchased people from every tribe, language, people, and nation?
3. What does the word *worthy* (5:2, 9) mean?

THE LAMB BREAKS THE SEALS (6:1–17)

In the breaking of each seal, a divine messenger of judgment is summoned to go out into the world. The rider on the white horse symbolizes military power. This rider is not the same as the "Word of God" who also rides a white horse in chapter 19:11. This rider starts a series of the Tribulation horrors, while the rider in 19:11 represents the victorious return of Jesus to defeat His enemies.

The second rider is on a blood-red horse and pictures a plunging of the world into a great war. The twentieth century brought the deaths of over one hundred million people in wars (fifty million in WW II alone!). Although mankind is advancing in technology, mass destruction has also advanced.

The third horse is black with a scale in the rider's hand. The image is of the famine and scarcity which comes through warfare. The cost of food has multiplied twelve times! Yet this famine is limited by God's mercy.

The fourth rider is on a pale horse. The color is most likely "cadaverous," and the rider is death personified. Hades is closely associated with death as the place where the dead go. This first series of judgments results in a global war over one-fourth of the earth which produces economic hardship, famine, and death.

The fifth seal gives a glimpse of Christian martyrs in heaven. These died for God's Word and His witness. To die in the Lord is to go to be with Him (Phil. 1:21–23). There is no "soul-sleep" but an immediate translation into

The vision of judgments poured out on the earth is modeled on the vision of Zechariah 6:1–8, where colored horses represent God's agents who execute His judgments on the rebellious nations.

Hades equals the Old Testament *Sheol* and is sometimes translated as "the grave," but it is not the final destiny for humans (cp. Rev. 20:13–14).

His presence. The martyrs are aware of what is transpiring on earth and they long for God's justice to be manifested. Each martyr is comforted and clothed by God in white, which symbolizes victory, honor, and righteousness (cp. 3:4; 7:9, 13; 19:8). But others still will die and join them as they anticipate God's consummation.

Many Old Testament passages refer to cosmic events that mark the end-time revelation of God (cp. Isa. 50:3; Jer. 10:10; Isa. 2:2, 10, 12–21; 13:10–13; Ezek. 32:7–8; Joel 2:31; 3:15; Zech. 14:1–6; Zeph. 1:14–18).

The breaking of the sixth seal brings great cosmic disturbances which herald the coming of the Day of the Lord or The Day of Christ. This "Day" is a time period to which both the Old Testament and New Testament continually look forward (Joel 2:31; Mal. 4:5; Isa. 2:12; Jer. 25:15; Dan. 2:28, 44). This is the time of the final establishment of justice and righteousness on earth. Sin will be punished and the nations will know God's sovereignty and His Messiah.

Star

Star in the original language does not mean a star in the scientific sense. It is a general term which covers meteorites, planets, as well as stars in the scientific sense. Most likely the usage here is like our "shooting stars" or meteor showers.

QUESTIONS TO GUIDE YOUR STUDY

1. What parallels are there between the events in this chapter with what Jesus predicted in Matthew 24?
2. What comfort can come to believers from the content of the fifth seal?
3. Why does humankind fear God's day? How can this fear be taken away?

THE 144,000 SEALED (7:1–8)

Chapter 7 is an interlude in the action, and it describes two significant groups. The first is the 144,000 who are sealed. Many different opinions are held on the identity of this group: Jehovah's Witnesses claim it is their group; some say it is the Church; others say it is converted Jewish people. Romans 11 predicts a future conversion of Israel, and the term *Israel* occurs sixty-eight times in the New Testament. All of the usages are of Jewish people. (Galatians 6:16 is no exception.) So the literal sense makes good sense. Doubtless in the last days the identification of God's people and God's enemies (the beast's people) will be evident (cp. Rev. 13:16–17). Economic and physical persecution will come to God's people, but divine wrath will be on those who receive Satan's mark. Just what these marks will be is not known.

THE GREAT MULTITUDE IN WHITE ROBES (7:9–17)

The second group in this chapter is a great multitude of people who come out of the Great Tribulation. These people are in heaven and so have died during this terrible period. How they die is not revealed here (cp. 17:6; 18:24; 19:2; 20:4), but they are killed for the faith. The Great Tribulation will be a period of great evangelization as well as of judgments. The ministry of the witnesses (described in chapter 11) is a 1,260-day-long event of signs and wonders with the Word that brings God's truth to the world. In addition, the nation of Israel may have a supernatural ministry to the Gentile world during this time (cp. Rom. 11:12, 25–26;

The background for this vision is Ezekiel 9:4, 6 where God's judgment does not fall on those with a mark on their foreheads.

possibly the 144,000; and Rev. 12:13–17). In Revelation 14:6–7, an angel warns the world of the need to know and worship God. The signs and cosmic disturbances (6:12–14) may also wake a sleepy world from its spiritual slumber. Many people will come to faith and many will die for their faith.

QUESTIONS TO GUIDE YOUR STUDY

1. What does the white robe mean in this vision?
2. What picture is given of heaven in this scene?
3. In what way are Christians sealed today and for what purpose (2 Cor. 1:22; Eph. 1:13; 4:30)?

THE SEVENTH SEAL AND THE TRUMPET JUDGMENTS (8:1–6)

The relationship of the seals, trumpets, and bowls judgments can be charted as follows:

Recapitulation View

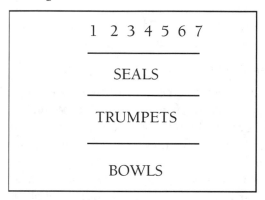

Linear View

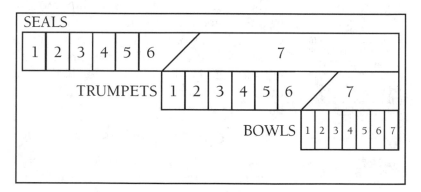

In the recapitulation view, the same judgments are described over and over again in increasing detail. In the linear view, each series of judgments is distinct and issues into the next series of more intense judgments. If the Tribulation is taken as a seven-year period or as a

Altar

In contrast to *bómos* which is used to describe pagan altars, the Septuagint (Greek Old Testament) is the first place where the *thysiastérion*, "sacrificial table," or altar occurs. It occurs in the Septuagint 419 times. In Revelation it occurs eight times.

Trumpets were used in Israel to summon the people to attention. They were often used to announce a battle or a solemn emergency. Joel 2:1 is typical: "Blow the trumpet in Zion; sound the alarm on my holy hill. Let all who live in the land tremble, for the day of the LORD is coming" (cp. Judg. 3:27; 7:8; Neh. 4:18; Ezek. 33:1).

Joel predicts similar signs before the final Day of the Lord: "I will show wonders in the heavens and on the earth, blood and fire and billows of smoke" (Joel 2:30).

three-and-one-half-year period, the difference is not too great. A linear view seems to be the simple reading of the text.

The trumpet judgments are introduced with solemnity. First there is a dramatic pause. Then seven angels prepare to execute God's will. Then another angel takes fire from the heavenly altar and casts it to earth. The judgment which comes is in response to the prayers of God's people, who long for His victory and His righteousness to be manifested.

THE FIRST TRUMPET (8:7)

The trumpet judgments have similarities to the plagues and judgments which God poured out on Egypt at the time of Israel's Exodus (Exod. 7–11). However, the trumpets signal much greater and universal disasters which are not confined to one nation. The purpose is similar: to warn, to punish, and to bring people to repentance and faith. Hail, fire, and blood come to the earth. Many understand the fire to be lightning. Blood-red rain does occur in places of volcanic activity or near the red sands from the Sahara Desert. The result of this first trumpet judgment is the destruction of a third of the earth's vegetation. This will greatly affect humanity's food supply.

THE SECOND TRUMPET (8:8–9)

As the second trumpet sounds, something like a gigantic meteorite crashes into the sea, causing a third of the sea to turn bloody (cp. Exod. 7:20). A third of sea life dies, and a third of the world's shipping is destroyed. Much of the world today depends on food supplies from other parts of the world, transported on the seas. Terrible economic disasters and suffering will take place.

THE THIRD TRUMPET (8:10–11)

Another heavenly body comes crashing down. This star (meteorite) is named "Wormwood" for its effect on the inland waters—the great rivers. All the water is polluted and many people die (cp. Jer. 9:14–15; 23:15).

THE FOURTH TRUMPET (8:12)

With the blowing of this trumpet, the Egyptian plague of darkness is recalled (Exod. 10:21–23). Sun, moon, and stars lose a third of their luminosity, so both day and night are darker.

The judgment of darkness is to warn the world to flee to Christ, who has come as light into the world (John 8:12). The great tragedy is that people often stay in the dark because their practices are evil (John 3:19–21). The final destiny of the rebellious is a place of outer darkness (Matt. 8:12; 22:13).

THE VISION OF THE FLYING EAGLE (8:13)

The word translated "eagle" may also be a "vulture" (some manuscripts have the word *angel* instead). The warning of the heavenly messenger is a threefold "woe" which corresponds to the next three trumpet judgments. The first four were upon the elements or nature. The last will be upon humanity. Jesus Himself warned, "Wherever there is a carcass, there the vultures [or eagles] will gather" (Matt. 24:28). Death is coming!

The plant in the ancient world called "wormwood" was not poisonous, but it was proverbial for its bitterness and so was used as a symbol for the bitter result of sin. Sin often is very pleasurable at first—with the outcome of bitterness and death. Thus, Deuteronomy 29:18 warns in the Hebrew language that the fruit of idolatry is "gall and wormwood" (KJV).

When Krakatoa, a volcano in Indonesia, exploded on August 27, 1883, nearly five cubic miles of rock and dust were thrown into the air. The surrounding region was dark for two and one-half days and dust drifted around the earth several times, causing bright red sunsets for a year. Something similar may happen with this series of judgments.

The fifth and sixth trumpet judgments use some common Old Testament and contemporary symbolism. In the fifth, there is a plague of locusts—a calamity which came all too often in the Middle East. In the sixth, there is a plague of horsemen similar to the Parthian warriors who threatened Rome from the East. The eighth plague of Egypt (Exod. 10:12–20) was the locusts, while Joel describes an army invasion in terms of locusts which is the clear background for this vision (Joel 1–2).

The visual description should not be pushed into excessive literalism. For example, Jesus is seen in chapter 1 with a long priestly garment. In chapter 6, He is the slain and victorious lamb or ram, while in chapter 19 He rides a white horse into battle with a sword coming out of His mouth. Each vision presents truth about Jesus' person and office, but we should not try to paint a picture of His physical nature.

THE FIFTH TRUMPET—FIRST WOE (9:1–12)

The plague of locusts in this vision is different than normal locusts. These seem demonic as they come up out of the "abyss" or bottomless pit. In Luke 8:31, the abyss is the place of demons. These locusts do not feed on vegetation like normal locusts, but they torture people for five months. Not everyone is under this plague. Like the later plagues of Egypt, the Lord makes a distinction between His people and those under judgment (Exod. 3:22–23). The believers are not appointed for wrath and they have a seal from God (7:1–8). The limitation of this plague to five months is a warning and an opportunity to repent. As terrible as this demonic plague is, people will not die from it, but they will wish they could.

The leader of the locusts is named "Destroyer." He is a fallen angel or demon and may be referred to in 2 Peter 2:4. The physical descriptions of these horrors are appalling—part human, part animal. It must be remembered that John was seeing a vision filled with symbols.

THE SIXTH TRUMPET (9:13–21)

At the border of the Roman Empire to the east was the River Euphrates. Beyond lived the Parthians, an Iranian people, who were a grave threat to the civilized world of Rome. Several times their mounted troops constituted a terror from the East. The plague of the sixth trumpet shows a similar imagery: (1) origin near the Euphrates River; (2) the bright-plated armor of the horses and riders; (3) the Parthian tactic of shooting a volley of arrows while charging and retreating (cp. 9:19).

In a number of end-time prophecies in the Bible, there are predictions of invasions from the East or the North. (Because of Israel's location, most invasions from the East circled the desert and came in from the North.) In the past history of the Jewish people, they had suffered from Assyrians, Babylonians, and Persians who invaded from the east and north. Ezekiel prophesied of an end-time invasion of Gog and Magog (38:1–39:16). In the pseudepigraphical book of 1 Enoch (56:5–7) a vision similar to Revelation 9:13–21 occurs:

> In those days, the angels will assemble and throw themselves down to the east at the Parthians and Medes. They will shake up the kings (so that) a spirit of unrest shall come upon them, and stir them up from their thrones; and they will break forth . . . like lions . . . like hyenas. And they will go up and trample upon the land of My elect ones, and the land of My elect ones will be before them like a threshing floor or a highway.

In the sixth plague, four angels (demonic) who were bound at the Euphrates are unleashed. The coming judgment is ordained to come at a precise time (9:15) marked out by God. The events set loose will bring the death of one-third of mankind. Previous disasters such as the flood on Noah or the black death of the Middle Ages are the only comparisons in history. The destructive forces consist of a cavalry of 200,000,000 horsemen. Some interpreters argue for literal armies from the East and point to China's militia. Others emphasize that these are demonic forces from hell and that literal human armies are not intended. The horses and their riders have elements like animals, like humans, and with fire, smoke, and sulfur (brimstone) that are hellish. As in the previous plague, the historical background is the Parthian cavalry. But these "horrible hordes" are demon-inspired and demon-led, resulting in unparalleled death and destruction.

As the plague comes upon the world, the two-thirds of humanity not killed might be expected to turn to the Lord in faith and repentance. But they are so enmeshed in their false religions that they do not see the truth. While it's true that "an idol is nothing at all in the world" (1 Cor. 8:4), demon forces are involved in false religions and they deceive people. In later visions of this book, satanic deceptions and false worship are described in more detail.

QUESTIONS TO GUIDE YOUR STUDY

1. How does God use angels (good) to work out His purposes?
2. How do Satan and the fallen angels (demons) fit into the plan of God?
3. What role do humans have in relation to angels (1 Cor. 4:9; 6:3; Heb. 2:5; Eph. 3:10)?
4. Why is it so hard for unbelievers to see God's grace?
5. What is the connection between faith and works?
6. What are some modern forms of idolatry?

Paul warned us that the god of this age (Satan) has "blinded the minds of unbelievers, so that they cannot see the light of the gospel of the glory of Christ" (2 Cor. 4:4). Not only do people hang on to their false worship, but they also continue in their wicked lifestyles. If the first part of the Ten Commandments is broken, then violations of the second tablet are sure to come. Love of God and love of humanity are linked. True biblical love for God is a response to His love for us (1 John 4:19). True biblical love for God has ethical results (1 John 4:7–8, 11, 20–21; Rom. 13:8–10).

THE MIGHTY ANGEL AND THE LITTLE SCROLL (10:1–7)

As the seventh trumpet is anticipated, another interlude takes place (cp. 7:1–8). The sounding of the trumpet is delayed until 11:14–19. In this interlude, another series of seven thunders is announced, but they are mysteriously sealed up and not revealed (cp. 2 Cor. 12:2–4). In this interlude, John tells of a great angel from heaven who gives him a little book to eat. He also records the measuring of the temple and the ministry of the two witnesses.

The mighty angel of Revelation is so glorious that some have thought him to be Jesus Himself. While the term *angel* is not decisive (for it can be used of men, spirit beings, or even of God), he seems to be one of a series of messengers (cp. 6:4; 5:2; 10:3). The angel takes a stance on land and sea with an uplifted arm. He announces that "there will be no more delay." (Not the end of "time" in a metaphysical sense.)

The great question is always "how long?" Now, heaven swears, the end of Satan's kingdom has come; God's kingdom will be established on earth. The restrainer of 2 Thessalonians 2:3 is removed and the prayers of the martyrs answered (Rev. 6:11). Since the time of Moses (c. 1400 B.C.), a long series of prophets have given predictions of the purpose of God in His Messiah without understanding the exact time sequences of suffering and glory (1 Pet. 1:10–12). The "mystery" is now to be fully made known because God is not only giving revelation but He is working out the actual events.

John's vision is full of Old Testament images and themes. On the angel, compare Daniel 8:16; 12:7. On the cloud, compare Psalm 104:3; Daniel 7:13; Acts 1:9. But the strongest similarities to this vision come from Ezekiel 1:26–28; 2:8–3:3. The angel has the very glory of the Lord upon him. Ezekiel was shown a scroll which was unrolled and full of lament, mourning, and woe. He was told to eat the scroll, and it was sweet in his mouth.

Paul, after explaining part of God's plan in Jew, Gentile, and church interactions (see Rom. 9–11), wrote: "Oh, the depth of the riches of the wisdom and knowledge of God! How unsearchable his judgments, and his paths beyond tracing out! 'Who has known the mind of the Lord? Or who has been his counselor?' 'Who has ever given to God, that God should repay him?' For from him and through him and to him are all things. To him be the glory forever! Amen" (Rom. 11:33–36).

As John, Ezekiel, and Jeremiah did—so we are to "eat" the Word of God and assimilate it into our being. As we meditate upon it, it will become "sweeter than honey" (Ps. 19:10) and more desirable than gold. But as Paul had continual sorrow and pain in his heart because of the unbelief of his people (Rom. 9:1–3), so we should have sorrow over the sin and unbelief in our nation.

JOHN CONSUMES THE SCROLL AND IS COMPELLED TO PROPHESY (10:8–11)

John is now commanded to take and eat a scroll. The content of this little scroll is about the completion of God's mystery which the prophets of the Old Testament proclaimed. This is a "mystery" because unless God discloses to humans what He is going to do, they will never be able to figure out His plan.

Several Old Testament prophets had an experience similar to John's. Ezekiel heard a voice and saw a hand outstretched to him with a written scroll. He was told to eat this scroll and it was sweet in his mouth (Ezek. 2:8–3:3). Jeremiah in a poetic passage declared:

> Your words were found, and I ate them,
>   and your words became to me a joy
>   and the delight of my heart (Jer. 15:16, NRSV).

Both Ezekiel and Jeremiah found that the messages of judgment which they had to deliver to the people caused a lot of pain for them. So John found the scroll "sweet as honey in my mouth, but when I had eaten it, my stomach turned sour" (v. 10). Why would the message be first sweet, then cause bitterness? Probably the answer is that all of God's revelation is as Psalm 119:103 says: "How sweet are your words to my taste, sweeter than honey to my mouth!"

Yet John's message contains elements of judgment, martyrdom, persecution, and eternal punishment. God Himself says that He takes no pleasure in the death of the ungodly or of anyone (Ezek. 18:32) but wants them to turn and live. He wants them to get a new heart and a new spirit! It is a bitter thing to contemplate the second death (Rev. 20:11–15).

John's commission is to prophesy again. The content is not certain, but it most likely contains the material of the later part of his book (Rev. 11–22).

■ *God, in His kindness, reveals His purposes*
■ *to people today in a written book. In the*
■ *past the revelation came in many ways,*
■ *including dreams, visions, and trances. To*
■ *have a written record of God's prophecy is a*
■ *great privilege.*

QUESTIONS TO GUIDE YOUR STUDY

1. What features make the angel in 10:1–4 impressive?
2. Why are the seven thunders sealed?
3. How certain is this prophecy?

Measuring the Temple

Ezekiel 40–42 describes the prophet watching a man measuring various parts of the Temple and its courts. The glory of the Lord returns to the Temple with the promise that this Temple will never be defiled again as the previous Temples had been by foreign invaders. Zechariah (2:1–13) also describes a measuring of the city of Jerusalem as a prelude to God's working for His people.

Martyrs, witness

A witness in legal terms testifies concerning what he has seen and heard. In biblical terms, the witness proclaims what he knows. Jesus is called the faithful and true witness (Rev. 1:15; 3:14). By the end of the first century, the name *martyrs* was given to the persons who sealed their testimony with their blood. So in Revelation 2:13 "Antipas, my faithful witness, who was put to death."

JOHN MEASURES THE TEMPLE (11:1–2)

John is given a bamboo-like cane and is told to measure the Temple. When we see people surveying, we normally think that a new building or a renovation will soon take place. Interpreters differ on the significance of this vision. The symbolic interpretations see the preservation of the church in this passage. The more literal interpretations see a fulfillment in the city of Jerusalem on the ancient temple site of Mount Moriah. They look forward to a rebuilding of the Jewish Temple and point to 2 Thessalonians 2:4. In this passage, Paul reminds Christians of a future desecration of the Temple. Jesus also warns of a sign in the future of an abomination that causes desolation (Mark 13:14; Matt. 24:15) in the holy place. John is writing down his prophecy after the destruction of the second Temple (Herod's) in A.D. 70. Most likely, his vision concerns the end-time temple.

THE TWO WITNESSES (11:3–14)

In 11:2, the Gentiles are to trample the holy city for forty-two months. This time notation is a reference to the prophecy of Daniel 9 which concerns "seventy weeks of years." The last seven years is divided into two segments and referred to in a number of passages. Sometimes the days are numbered as 1,260 (three years of thirty-day months). Sometimes a period of tribulation is said to be "a time, times and half a time" (Dan. 7:25; 12:7). This same period is found in Revelation 12:6, 14; 13:5.

The two witnesses are two end-time prophets whom God will raise up. They remind us of Moses (the miracles) and Elijah (the miracles and three-year judgment). They prophesy in sackcloth or mourning garments. These garments were of a coarse material and were often black, to distinguish them from normal clothing. They had supernatural power and protection. They minister most likely during the first three years of the period, known as Daniel's seventieth week. Many interpreters take a symbolic interpretation and see this fulfilled in the church. A more literal interpretation sees the fulfillment in the land of Israel during the last days. The city where Christ was crucified is Jerusalem (11:8), and it is a bit of a stretch to see this city as Babylon or Rome or Egypt. The mention of "Sodom and Egypt" refers to both as the enemies of God with their immorality, slavery, and idolatry.

At the completion of their witness to God, they become martyrs. They are killed by the beast (or the Antichrist as he is known). This end-time person is a main character in the book of Revelation and is the same as the "man of sin" mentioned by Paul in 2 Thessalonians 2. To let a body lie in the streets of a city was a terrible dishonor during biblical times. A devil's Christmas celebration takes place as people rejoice in their opposition to God's message and messengers. But their joy turns to terror as the witnesses are resurrected and taken before their eyes to heaven. A judgment of an earthquake occurs which kills many people but also causes repentance toward God. This event may be significant in the conversion of the Jews during the Tribulation.

Olive trees and lampstands

In Zechariah 4, a vision of a lampstand and olive trees representing the testimony and power of God is seen. The olive trees are two men selected to do the work of rebuilding the Temple.

- **Even as the Gentiles trampled the city of**
- **Jerusalem, God did not forget His ancient**
- **people (Rom. 11:28–29). He raised up two**
- **prophets to witness to the nation.**

THE SEVENTH TRUMPET (11:15–19)

The seventh angel blew his trumpet. With this trumpet blast, the earthly establishment of God's kingdom is announced. This concludes the series which began in chapter 8 (cp. vv. 6, 10, 12, 13). The content of chapters 10:1–11:13 are parenthetical. No immediate content of the seventh trumpet is revealed, but the seven bowl judgments are the content. Before John describes the events which will bring in the King with His kingdom, more parenthetical revelation is given about the actors in this great drama of history (chaps. 12–14).

The response of heaven is first given. Later both humankind's and nature's response is revealed (vv. 18–19). Heaven solemnly proclaims that "the kingdom of the world" has become the kingdom of God and of His Messiah. The theme of the kingdom is a major theme of the Bible if not the very center of biblical theology. The kingdom was the message of John the Baptist and of Jesus (Matt. 3:2; 4:23).

A kingdom is the sphere or realm over which a ruler exercises his authority. The realm can be physical, spiritual, or both. In the political realm, the Jewish people achieved a significant kingdom under David and his son Solomon (2 Sam. 5:1–1 Kings 11). But because of disobedience, the Jewish political state was reduced and placed in servitude to various pagan nations—Assyrians, Babylonians, Persians, Greeks, and Romans. The people of Jesus' day longed for freedom from the Gentile or pagan domination (cp. Luke 1:68–75; John 6:14; and Acts 1:6).

The great mistake for Israel was its tendency to forget the spiritual realm and to think that political deliverance was all-important. As early as the foundation of the Hebrew monarchy, the people rejected God's rule and demanded an earthly solution to their troubles (1 Sam. 8:1–22). The spiritual realm is more important than the human or political kingdom. The Bible opens our minds to spiritual forces and realms of which we would be totally ignorant if God didn't reveal them to us. Behind earthly kingdoms are spiritual powers headed by one who is called the *archon* or ruler of this world.

Jesus faced this individual in His temptation (Matt. 4:1–11). This *archon* offered Jesus "all the kingdoms of the world." Jesus, in obedience, conquered Satan (the *archon*) (John 12:31; 14:30; 16:11). Today, while the decisive battle has been won on the Cross, there is still the "mopping-up operation." The world system lies under the control of the wicked one (1 John 5:19).

Jesus came into the world of darkness to destroy the works of the devil (1 John 3:8). Satan has a spiritual kingdom of darkness (1 John 3:14; Col. 1:13), as well as control over the physical kingdoms of this world. Paul wrote that the "god of this age" blinds the minds of people so they do not see "the light of the gospel of the glory of Christ, who is the image of God" (2 Cor. 4:4).

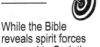

While the Bible reveals spirit forces opposed to God, the believer is not to fear (cp. 2 Kings 6:16). There are "more with us" than with the enemies of God. John encouraged his people by reminding us that "the one who is in you [God in the person of the Holy Spirit] is greater than the one who is in the world" (1 John 4:4). The major message of the book of Revelation is the triumph of God over evil in this world.

Psalm 2 describes the long conflict between God's rule and pagan insurrection. The psalm first reveals the revolt against the anointed king of Israel. But God laughs at the insolence and firmly establishes His kingdom. Jesus as David's Son faced the same opposition and rejection. The New Testament quotes this psalm in reference to Jesus as God's Messiah (cp. Acts 4:25; 13:33; Heb. 1:5; 5:5).

Revelation 11:15 states that the Messiah will reign forever when He takes over the kingdom of the world. When Jesus was born, the angel Gabriel told Mary that her Son would have David's throne and that He would rule forever and His kingdom would never end (Luke 1:32–33). The angelic promise embraces a number of Old Testament predictions. In 2 Samuel 7:15, David is promised that his lineage will be established forever. In Daniel 2:44, God predicts a kingdom which will destroy the Gentile world empires, and in Daniel 7:14, 28, the prediction is of a messianic eternal kingdom. The one-thousand-year reign of Christ in Revelation 20:4–6 and in 1 Corinthians 15:24–28 is best understood as the initial phase of God's eternal kingdom.

In 11:16 the heavenly beings—the twenty-four elders—prostrate themselves in worship before God at the wonder of His coming rule. The angels in heaven must be puzzled over the whole drama of redemption. Two references in the epistles seem to teach this. Peter said, "Even angels long to look into these things" (1 Pet. 1:12). And Paul revealed that the church is an object lesson of God's grace to heavenly beings (Eph. 3:10). The incarnation of our Lord was an act of grace in which He took on humanity, "for surely it is not angels he helps, but Abraham's descendants" (Heb. 2:16). Although there is angelic sin (see Rev. 12:7), yet there is no revelation of salvation for angels.

The coming of the King with His kingdom means that He will rule in righteousness. Rebellion will be put down and punished, and rewards will be given for those who have been loyal to the King. The Old Testament "Day of the Lord" is the time when God will come and visit His people in judgment (Isa. 2:1–4; Joel 1:15; Amos 5:18–24; Mal. 4:1–6). The rewards given to God's faithful are in this world (Rev. 3:10) but mainly in the resurrection or in heaven (cp. Jesus' beatitudes, Matt. 5:2–10 and Rev. 2:7, 10, 17, 28; 3:5, 21; Rev. 21:13). In Revelation 11:18–19, the nations are angry at the kingdom of God while nature displays its awe before the Lord in lightning, thunder, hail, and earthquake.

- *The final series of judgments is announced.*
- *The long-awaited kingdom is coming to*
- *earth with Jesus the King.*

QUESTIONS TO GUIDE YOUR STUDY

1. Why is Jerusalem the city of importance?
2. How could the whole world see the dead bodies of the martyrs?
3. Why would people follow the Antichrist and refuse to respond to God's prophets?
4. Why do the angels fall on their faces before God? Review Old Testament visitations of God to humans.
5. Why has the kingdom taken so much time to be established on earth?
6. Why should we pray for the coming of the kingdom (cp. Matt. 6:10)?

REVELATION 12

The word *sign* (*sêmeion*) is an organizing theme of the Gospel of John (cp. John 2:11; 4:54; 6:2; 7:31; 11:47; 12:18, 37; 20:30).

The vision seems like a myth rather than an historical account. Although many pagan myths have similar motifs, the birth of Jesus and the opposition of Satan really occur in our world and datable history. C. S. Lewis has written helpful material on the "true myth" or the mythical becoming historical ("on myth" in *An Experiment in Criticism*, 1961; cp. *C. S. Lewis: Defender of the Faith* by Richard Cunningham, 1967, pp. 141–200; "The Myth of Deep Heaven" in *The Christian World of C. S. Lewis* by Clyde S. Kilby, 1964, pp. 79–116; especially "Myth, Fact, and Truth," pp. 93–99 in *C. S. Lewis: Apostle to the Skeptics* by Chad Walsh, 1949). Thus, a myth can be a literary form like an allegory and used to depict historical truth.

THE WOMAN, THE CHILD, AND THE DRAGON (12:1–6)

This next section is most unusual. John usually introduces new visions with expressions like "I saw" (1:12), "after this I saw" (4:1), "and I saw" (5:1; 6:1, 12). Here he sees the appearance of a "sign" in heaven.

Here the word *sign* seems to have the sense of a striking phenomenon or a portent. The sign is a brilliant woman and the reader of the Bible would naturally connect the image to the dream of Joseph in Genesis 37:9. If this is correct, the woman has something to do with Israel. The identity of the great red dragon is clearly revealed in verse 9 as Satan or the devil. The identity of the man-child (v. 5) is clearly the Messiah since the text uses the language of the second Psalm, verse 9, where it indicated that God's Messiah "will rule [all nations] with an iron scepter." This expression occurs in Revelation at 2:27 and 19:15. In the first passage, Jesus is sharing His rule with His people. In the second, Jesus is returning as the conquering Messiah.

The section (12:1–6) may be understood in this way. Israel, the woman, after a long pregnancy, finally gives birth to the Messiah—the man-child—who will rule. The great cosmic struggle between good and evil, God and Satan, which is described in brief in the next section, is seen here on earth.

Satan (v. 9) is pictured in this vision as a great red dragon with seven heads and ten horns. In 17:9, the last world empire is described in similar language. The terminology of beasts, heads, and horns is based on Daniel 7:1–28 and Zechariah 1:18–21. The dragon is similar to the pictures in the Old Testament of monsters who are enemies of God and His people (Isa. 27:1; Ps. 74:12–14; Ps. 89:9–10). The biblical picture of Satan is of a fallen angel who has great but limited power. He is an opponent of God and His people, seeking to destroy God's work (cp. Matt. 4:1–11; 1 Pet. 5:8–9). He is called the "prince of this world" (or ruler, Gk. *archon*) by Jesus (John 14:30), and John declared that the whole world is under his control.

Satan's opposition to God is manifested in hatred of His servants, and he attempts to destroy the child at His birth (v. 4). It is easy to see why many interpreters see Satan at work in Herod's attempt to kill the infant Jesus (Matt. 22:1–18). Since the devil was foiled in his efforts to destroy the Redeemer who is taken to heaven, he turns to attack the woman who gave birth. She flees into the wilderness where God preserves her. The reference is to God's protection of His people (most likely converted Jews in the Tribulation) during Daniel's three and one-half years (9:27). This period is the same as in 7:1–8; 11:3–10; 13:5–8.

■ *The great battle between God and Satan is*
■ *revealed in picture form with God's miracu-*
■ *lous protection of His people.*

WAR IN HEAVEN—SATAN CAST OUT—WRATH ON EARTH (12:7–12)

The Bible is clear about the outcome of the great cosmic struggle. The devil and his angels are doomed. Jesus says they will go into eternal fire

Satan's titles

In the Bible, Satan is called the great red dragon, the deceiver of the world, the wicked one, the *archon* of the world, Lucifer, the tempter, the old serpent, the prince of darkness, the adversary, the accuser of the brothers, the father of lies, Beelzebub, the prince of the power of the air, the father of the children of evil.

As Paul writes, "Who will bring any charge against God's elect? It is God who justifies. Who is to condemn? It is Christ Jesus, who died . . . and who was raised" (Rom. 8:33–34; see Rom. 8:31; 3:21–31; 2 Cor. 5:19–21; 1 John 2:1–2). Our sins are "imputed" to Jesus on the cross and His righteousness is "imputed" (or "credited to our account") to us. The accuser now has nothing to accuse against us. Jesus has put it all to His account and settled it once for all with His mighty shout from the cross: "*Tetelestai*"—"it is finished!" (John 19:30).

which has been prepared for them (Matt. 25:41). John sees the devil, the beast, and the false prophet all thrown into the lake of fire and sulfur, where they will remain forever. But in the revelation to John, he is shown part of a great mystery: war in heaven!

Two great archangels with their hosts go into battle. Michael ("who is like God") is an archangel mentioned in Daniel as a guardian of the Jewish people (12:1; 10:13, 21), and in the book of Jude (v. 9), he "contended with the devil and disputed about the body of Moses" (NRSV). How angels could sin and how there could be a battle in heaven are unknown to us. Satan is pictured as defeated—but not by Michael's great power. As in the book of Jude where the Lord rebukes Satan, so here victory is the Lord's. By His death and resurrection, Jesus has defeated Satan and his hosts.

The overthrow of Satan's kingdom and the coming to earth of the messianic kingdom is announced again by a heavenly voice. In the Bible, Satan has many titles and descriptions. His two principle names are "Satan" (Hebrew, "accuser" or "adversary") and "devil" (Greek, "slanderer"). Peter warns Christians about "your adversary the devil" (1 Pet. 5:8, NRSV). Somehow Satan has a perverted sense which points out the flaws and sins—real or possible—in God's people (cp. Job 1–2; Zech. 3:1–5). In the Revelation 12:10 passage, heaven is rejoicing at the overthrow of the "accuser of our brothers." God's people in heaven are ecstatic over the victory won by the blood of the Lamb. What does this mean? By Jesus' death on the cross, human sin is now "atoned for." God's "rightness" is vindicated and His righteousness is granted as a gift to those who trust the finished work of Jesus.

- *The victory of Jesus on the cross and His*
- *resurrection ensure the defeat of Satan.*
- *God's people rejoice in heaven, but Satan is*
- *about to turn earth into a living hell.*

THE DRAGON PERSECUTES THE WOMAN AND HER CHILDREN (12:13–17)

When Satan is confined to the earth, his activities are intensified against humanity and his fury is unleashed because he knows he has only a limited time (12:12). Jesus has come to destroy the works of the devil (1 John 3:8) and to deliver people from Satan, who keeps people in bondage through fear of death (Heb. 2:14). Jesus has come as the "stronger one" and raided Satan's house and kingdom (Matt. 12:29; Col. 1:13).

The woman represents converted Israel (Rom. 11:26–27), or perhaps as Barnhouse held, "The woman represents all the saved of God from the time of Eve who received the promise that her seed would bruise the serpent's head" (*Revelation*, p. 229). She is now the object of Satan's wrath. Today God's people come out from mainly Gentile origins, but in the Tribulation a great number will be from Jewish origins, for that time is called Jacob's trouble (Jer. 30:7). The 144,000 Israelites of 7:4–8 is another indication of a large scale turning to Jesus during the Tribulation.

Right from the beginning of the Hebrew nation, as God was freeing Israel from Egypt, Pharaoh and his host sought to destroy the infant nation. God reminded His people of His salvation in Exodus 19:4 (NASB):

"You yourselves have seen what I did to the Egyptians, and how I bore you on eagles' wings, and brought you to Myself."

So in the Tribulation God will protect His people in their wilderness experience for the period of forty-two months or "a time, times and half a time" (cp. Dan. 7:25). Satan's failure will result in his turning to attack God's faithful throughout the whole world. The reference to the floodwater and the earth helping the woman (12:15–16) brings to mind the sea parting for Israel so they could cross on dry ground and escape their enemies.

■ *Persecution of God's people will be rampant,*
■ *but God knows how to protect and deliver*
■ *His own in the midst of their troubles.*

QUESTIONS TO GUIDE YOUR STUDY

1. Why is Satan so opposed to the man-child?
2. Why does John use this picture language?
3. How has Satan been at work in modern times?
4. Why is Satan opposed to Christians?
5. How does Satan deceive the whole world (12:9)?
6. What will the devil's wrath produce on earth (12:12)?
7. Where and why are Christians being persecuted today?
8. What do Christians learn in persecution?
9. In what ways has Satan attacked the Jewish people?

REVELATION 13

THE BEAST OUT OF THE SEA (13:1–4)

Following the frustration of Satan in chapter 12, the dragon takes his stand on the sand of the sea (12:18). He almost seems to be pondering his next strategy. The sea is often a symbol for the people (Isa. 57:20–21; Rev. 17:15). But perhaps here John sees this beast come out of the Mediterranean Sea. The beasts of Daniel's book are world empires: Babylon, Medo-Persia, Greece, and Rome. The last two were distinctively Mediterranean-based world powers. As John sees his visions and writes his Revelation, the ruling world empire is Rome. Almost all interpreters see the Roman Empire reflected in some way in this book. But since Rome is no longer a world power, how is this to be understood?

Explanations include a revival of the Roman Empire with the European Union or the Common Market developing into something sinister. Others see Rome as the Roman Catholic Church developing into the beast. Still others see the rise of Islam around the Mediterranean Sea and its developing into a major world power as it was in its early days. At least ten Islamic powers ring the sea with hatred for the state of Israel.

The beast is like the leopard, the bear, and the lion of Daniel's three world empires, and it is energized and characterized by the dragon (13:1–4, 12:3). In the Tribulation period, a final world power hostile to God will arise and demand to be worshiped. Deification of a human leader and an anti-Christian state have occurred with Hitler and Germany, Stalin and Russia, and Mao and China. The "beast" in John's vision has a

Beasts in the Old Testament

In the book of Daniel, visions of world empires hostile to God's people are seen as "beasts" or animals (Dan. 7:1–12; 17–18; 19–28; 8:1–27). "Horns" on the "beasts" are often symbols of other kings or kingdoms that develop (Dan. 8:22–23; 7:24–25). The "horns" are symbols of their power (Zech. 1:18–21; Rev. 17:12).

As this booklet is being written, neither Russia, nor Islam, nor a European Federation seems likely candidate for the beast as they perhaps once did. The anti-Catholics point to the past when Rome under Innocent III (1160–1216) dominated the European rulers and claimed the right of investiture of the emperor. Islam once ruled a unified kingdom from Tours, France, all around the Mediterranean Sea to Vienna. Hitler would have been a great candidate for the satanic beast in 1941–42 when he ruled Europe and a good part of North Africa. He also deified himself and placed an earthly authority over the church. Mass rallies exalted the leader, and even university professors had to begin their classes with a "Heil Hitler." The "Heil Hitler" could be as harmless as the English expression "God save the king" or as sinister as "Salvation is from Hitler."

remarkable power of recuperation as it has a "fatal wound" but survives. John will receive more information on this beast from an angel in chapter 17 (vv. 7–18).

This satanic kingdom will have worldwide power—"And the whole earth was amazed and followed after the beast" (Rev. 13:3, NASB).

Prediction is perilous. But the Bible does warn us of one called the Antichrist (1 John 2:18). Paul calls him the "man of sin" and the "son of perdition" (2 Thess. 2:3, KJV), and the "lawless one" (2 Thess. 2:8). He is probably the "little horn" of Daniel 7:8–12, 21–22, 24–28, and perhaps the "ruler who will come" of Daniel 9:26.

The beast out of the sea will be given great power and authority by Satan. The leader of this beastly kingdom will be a human but he will be empowered by Satan himself. Paul said of him: "He will oppose and will exalt himself over everything that is called God or is worshiped, so that he sets himself up in God's temple, proclaiming himself to be God" (2 Thess. 2:4).

- *At the end of this age, the beast or the Antichrist will arise with great satanic power. He*
- *is foreshadowed in the Roman Empire and*
- *other tyrannical dictator states.*

THE REIGN AND THE WORSHIP OF THE BEAST (13:5–10)

The beast will speak arrogantly and mouth blasphemies. Verse 13:5 is clearly built on Daniel 7:8, 20, 25 where the "little horn" speaks boastfully and wars against God's people for three and one-half years. So the beast reigns forty-two months and starts a great persecution in which many are killed for the faith. This satanically empowered person will become a world ruler as the devil's vice-regent (John 12:31; 14:30; 16:11). He will achieve what no tyrant has been able to accomplish—a universal dominion with universal worship. All will bow in submission to this person and his rule except God's elect ones. The refusal to go along with this world system will cost the lives of those who take a stand for God and His Messiah (cp. 15:2; 12:11; 7:14).

The solemn warning, "He who has an ear, let him hear" (13:9) is a call to spiritual perception for all to heed. God's people are to understand that the bitter persecution from the evil one is within the loving providence of the Father. For those who side with Satan, they are warned of the certainty of God's judgment which is to come soon. "Patient endurance" and "faithfulness" on the part of the Christian are necessary (cp. Gal. 5:22; Rom. 5:3, 4; Rev. 14:12).

■ *The Antichrist will rule and be worshiped*
■ *around the world. Christians will die rather*
■ *than worship the false god.*

THE BEAST FROM THE LAND (13:11–18)

Satan is a counterfeit in many of his ways. Here we see a satanic trinity: the dragon, the beast, and the false prophet. John sees a second beast similar to the first but subservient to the first. He comes from the "land" (earth) which may mean Israel. This beast parodies the Lamb who was slain (Rev. 5:6) as well as the Holy Spirit, for he is a false prophet (Rev. 20:10) who guides and directs the end-time false worship. This false prophet is analogous to the emperor in the emperor cult of the Roman Empire. People were forced to sacrifice to an image of the emperor.

The false prophet uses wondrous signs which deceive people into thinking that this is the true religion. Long ago Moses warned of false prophets with signs who would try to turn people away from the true God (Deut. 13:1–3). Paul said that the "man of sin" "will be in accordance with the work of Satan displayed in all kinds of counterfeit miracles, signs and wonders, and in every sort of evil that deceives those who are perishing" (2 Thess. 2:9–10).

Just as the magicians of Egypt could imitate some of Moses' signs, so this false prophet will simulate impressive signs much as the true witnesses did during the first three and one-half years of the Tribulation (Rev. 11:5–6). In a spectacular event, this prophet will imitate Elijah and bring down fire from heaven in "full view of men" (Rev. 13:13). In a world plugged into television and the Internet, the world will be mesmerized by this display of power and seduced by this false prophet. Undoubtedly, he will prepare the way for the satanic messiah. Jesus Himself predicted the coming of "false Christs and false prophets," and they "will show great signs and wonders, so as to mislead, if possible, even the elect" (Matt. 24:24, NASB).

Once the Antichrist has gained power, all tolerance will disappear. The false prophet will require a mark on the right hand or the forehead which will be a sign of ownership and of allegiance to the beast. The opposite will be the "seal" of the 144,000 (Rev. 7:4–8) which is the mark of the Father's ownership (Rev. 14:1–3). The one without the beast's mark will be unable to "buy or to sell." The Antichrist will have effective economic control of the world.

The "number" of the beast is a mystery. Many languages, including Hebrew, Aramaic, and Greek, used the letters of the alphabet for numerals (before the Arabic numbers). So every name would have a numerical calculation. Thus, 666 = "Nero Caesar" in Hebrew but not in Greek, which is the language The Revelation was written in. Many attempts have been made to link 666 with a great variety of persons: Nimrod (Gen. 10:8) the founder of Babylon, Napoleon, Mussolini, and many contemporaries, including Henry Kissinger and Social Security numbers! As the time approaches, the mark of allegiance to the beast will become obvious.

QUESTIONS TO GUIDE YOUR STUDY

1. Why is the Antichrist called a "beast"?
2. How does the beast of Revelation 13:1–4 relate to Daniel 7?
3. Where do we see deification of the state and its ruler in the world today?
4. How important is it for the Christian to be a nonconformist in the world (Rom. 12:1–2)?
5. How will the Antichrist win universal rule?
6. How can persecution of believers fit with Romans 8:28?
7. What are the signs of true prophets and of false prophets?
8. How could a "sign" be seen around the world (13:13)?
9. Early Christians faced a simple test: burn incense to Caesar or die. How important is it for you to live? Which sign will you live under or die for?

- *A satanic trinity will deceive the whole world*
- *and dominate it in economics and in religion.*
- *Opposition to these evil forces will mean*
- *death.*

REVELATION 14

THE SONG OF THE 144,000 (14:1–5)

In stark contrast to the satanic trinity of chapter 13, this vision shows the true Messiah and His people. In Psalm 2, God laughs at the insolence of those who oppose His people (2:4). And then in His anger He announces His resolve: "I have set my king on Zion, my holy hill" (2:6, NRSV). The Lamb is a symbol of Jesus the Messiah (John 1:29; Rev. 5:6, 12, 13; Isa. 53:7). The 144,000 (see notes on 7:1–8) are the same group seen in chapter 7, and they share in the victory of the Lord along with the great multitude (7:9–14). These come out of the Great Tribulation and have been redeemed. Their deliverance is marked out in a new song that Israel sang when they experienced salvation (Exod. 15:1; Pss. 40:1–3; 98:1–9).

The 144,000 are special soldiers of the Lamb who are committed to purity. This purity may be a symbol of absentation from fornication with the prostitute Babylon (cp. 17:1–2, 4; 18:3, 9). It could also be literal celibacy during the end-time when even marriage might be ill-advised because of the rampant corruption. Most Protestants react against any form of celibacy as a Roman Catholic teaching and a violation of God's plan (Gen. 2:18) and His apostle's warning ("they forbid marriage"; 1 Tim. 4:3, NRSV). Yet in times of crisis—such as holy war (Deut. 23:9; 1 Sam. 21:5; 2 Sam. 11:11)—celibacy may be necessary. John the Baptist, Jesus, and Paul renounced marriage because of a more important commitment (cp. 1 Cor. 7:1, 8, 26–40) or the crisis of the times.

Both the Old and New Testament point out the significance of Mount Zion which is the holy Temple mountain in Jerusalem. "Zion" appears to include Mount Moriah—the Temple site. Zion is the place of salvation of the Lord (cp. Joel 2:1; 3:16; Mic. 4:1–2; Zech. 1:14; 14:1–21; Ps. 132:13–14, 17–18; Heb. 12:22; Gal. 4:25–26; Isa. 2:2–4; 24:21–23).

How is your "song life?" Our salvation should bring forth songs of joy and of praise!

The discipleship of the 144,000 is unconditional and comprehensive. They are model Christians with unblemished character. They have "no lie" in them while the mass of humanity will embrace "the lie" (2 Thess. 2:9–11). They will be special "first fruits" of the great harvest of salvation which will take place during the Tribulation (cp. Rev. 7:9–13).

ANGELIC ANNOUNCEMENTS (14:6–12)

In rapid succession, John sees three angels flying one after another making announcements. The first tells everyone on earth the sovereign Creator is about to judge the world. Man's day is over and the Day of the Lord has come. This message is not exactly the good news of the grace of God in Jesus' death and resurrection (cp. 1 Cor. 15:3–5). By this time, the special ministry of the two witnesses and of the 144,000 will have made the issue clear. Also the world will have faced the decision about God's mark or Satan's mark. God's judgment is good news, for His justice will be manifested on earth.

The second angel announced the doom of Babylon. This is the first mention of "Babylon" in this book, but in the coming chapters much will be said. The doom of Babylon will be explained in the detailed visions of chapters 17 and 18.

The third messenger proclaims doom on the Antichrist and his followers. Babylon has given a cup of stupefying wine to the world, and they are drunk from its false teachings. The angel shouts with a loud voice to awaken humanity from its stupor. Those who worship the beast will have another cup to drink—God's wrath. The issues have eternal outcomes: the saints who are in the midst of the Tribulation are called to endurance and faith in Jesus.

Babylon

"Babel" or "Babylon" was one of the cities founded by Nimrod (Gen. 10:10). It became a symbol of man's pride and of his fall. Babylon was one of the major enemies of Israel, and they destroyed the Jerusalem Temple in 586 B.C. Zechariah 5:5–11 sees the land of Shinar (Babylon) as the site for wickedness. Daniel also lived in Babylon and experienced its oppression (chaps. 1–4). Interpreters of Revelation differ on whether "Babylon" will be rebuilt or if John is speaking of Rome or "a revived Rome."

- *The great tribulation will come to an end*
- *with the return of Jesus to Zion and the*
- *destruction of the kingdom of the Antichrist.*
- *Rewards and judgment will be given.*

What Happens at Death?

1. We will be with the Lord (Phil. 1:23).
2. We will be rewarded (Rev. 14:13).
3. We will be freed from earthly pain and problems (Rev. 7:17).

THE VISION OF THE GREAT HARVEST AND GOD'S WINEPRESS (14:13–20)

Prior to the vision is the second "beatitude" of this book. Commitment to Jesus will result in death. But death for the believer is to be with the Lord and to be rewarded. It will also bring the end to toil in the Tribulation period.

In the vision, Jesus "the Son of Man" receives word from an angel that everything is ready for the harvest judgment. The first reaping is the grain and the second is the grapes. The picture of the reaping or the harvest is a common biblical figure for the final judgment of the earth (Hos. 6:11; Joel 3:13; Jer. 51:33). After the grape harvest, the grapes would go into a winepress. People would trample the grapes in a winepress and the juice would flow out into a lower vat.

In this picture of judgment, human blood instead of grape juice flows out. Both Isaiah and Joel develop this terrible figure (Isa. 63:1–7; Joel 3:13). The flow of blood is beyond our imagination. It covers the entire land of Palestine to the depth of four feet! Some commentators spend too much time in literal calculations. This is a vision. We should not expect the beast to have seven literal heads nor should we expect to see Satan as an enormous red dragon. In a similar way, the winepress judgment will be part of the

Megiddo was a famous ancient city at the southern edge of the plain of Jezreel where many bloody battles were fought.

great final bloody battle known as Armageddon or Megiddo (cp. Rev. 16:14–16).

■ *Jesus with His angels will judge the rebel-*
■ *lious nations in a final great battle.*

QUESTIONS TO GUIDE YOUR STUDY

1. What are the characteristics of a disciple today?
2. Is Christian discipleship an optional activity?
3. How does discipleship relate to salvation?
4. Why do you think God uses the figures of the harvest and the winepress to describe the judgment of the nations?
5. In Isaiah 63, who is coming in judgment?
6. How should this passage motivate Christians today?

THE PRELUDE TO THE SEVEN BOWL JUDGMENTS (15:1–8)

The book of Revelation now moves to detailed descriptions of the judgments. Chapter 15 is a prelude. Chapter 16 unfolds the seven bowl judgments. Chapters 17 and 18 are visions of the doom of "Babylon the Great" and of the beast. Chapter 19 reveals the return of the Lord to defeat the hosts of the beast and the kings of the earth in the last battle.

The final series of judgments are called the "bowl judgments" because in the vision, John sees seven angels with "bowls." These bowls are full of the last plagues or judgments which will be poured out upon the rebellious nations and the world system. The bowl judgments are similar to the plagues of the Exodus which were poured out on the nation of Egypt. The "sea of glass mixed with fire" (v. 2) which the victors stand on seems to have some analogy to Israel's Exodus deliverance. The victors have gone through this into heaven. The cost of their victory has been their earthly lives, but like Israel's crossing of the sea they now have a song of deliverance. The song is called the song of Moses and the Lamb. It unites the people of God in the worship of God.

The song celebrates the "rightness" or justice of God as well as His holiness in the coming judgments. Sin and evil need to be destroyed. In the forbearance of God, He has not immediately punished human sin (cp. Rom. 3:25–26; 2 Pet. 3:9). A long period elapsed before Jesus came the first time to die for our sin (2 Cor. 5:17–21). Another long period has passed in which Jesus'

The Greek word *fiale* for "bowl" is specifically a bowl used in offerings. God's judgments are righteous and holy. They are seen to come from the heavenly Temple (cp. Rev. 5:8; 16:1; 15:6).

The World

Although John's favorite term for our world is *kosmos*, the actual word occurs only three times (Rev. 11:15, 13:8, 17:8). In contrast, the word *kosmos* occurs 94 times in his Gospel and 24 times in his epistles. Of the 186 usages of *kosmos* in the NT, John uses it 121 times. A common theological definition for this word is "that organized system that leaves God out." Today that includes governments, laws, economic systems, the entertainment industry, and our educational system. In Revelation 11:15 the kingdom of the *kosmos* comes to the rightful ruler—Jesus Christ.

sacrifice has been ignored or rejected, and evil has seemed to have free reign. Nevertheless, God will judge the *world* in righteousness.

The holiness and justice of God in His judgments is pictured in a number of details. First is the content of the song (vv. 3–4). The second is the opening of the heavenly sanctuary which normally, by analogy, only the high priest entered on earth. Third, the angels are wearing the marks of royal dignity and holiness. Fourth, the sanctuary is filled with smoke. The smoke pictures the awesome power of the glory of God (cp. Exod. 19:18; Isa. 6:4). At the giving of the law, Mount Sinai quaked and was covered in smoke in the presence of Yahweh. Isaiah had a similar revelation in his commission with the Temple shaking and filling with smoke. The high priests could not enter the inner sanctuary without a concealing cloud of smoke of the incense from the altar covering the mercy seat. Violation meant death (Lev. 16:12–13).

■ *God will judge the world system because of*
■ *His holiness and righteousness.*

QUESTIONS TO GUIDE YOUR STUDY

1. How do God's people conquer the beast?
2. How do songs function in the book of Revelation?
3. What is the role of the "four living creatures" in the book of Revelation?

THE SEVEN ANGELS WITH THE SEVEN LAST PLAGUES—THE BOWL JUDGMENTS (16:1–21)

The first bowl judgment is a plague of sores on those who worship the beast. In the sixth plague on Egypt (Exod. 9:10–11) "festering boils" broke out on both humans and animals. The Egyptian magicians could not stand before Moses because of their boils. So all those with the mark of the beast now have additional distinguishing marks! God also announced to His people in the Old Testament (Deut. 28:58–61) that the rejection of His revelation would be visited by "severe and lasting afflictions and grievous and lasting maladies" (NRSV). While this first plague is exceedingly painful, it is not fatal. It is a warning to the world to repent.

The second plague is on the sea, and it corresponds to the first Egyptian plague in which the Nile River "changed into blood" (Exod. 7:17–18). The fish in the Nile died and it began to stink. Its water was unfit to drink. So in this judgment the water becomes like the putrefaction of a dead person's blood. No more vile object exists for a Jewish observer like John. He sees the deadly stench of corruption spreading and life in the sea dying. If this is a universal judgment upon all the oceans, the human suffering will be enormous, for humans are dependent upon the oceans for food.

The third bowl is poured out on the inland waters or the fresh water supplies. Without fresh water, human life comes quickly to an end. Rejection of the blood of the Lamb—rejection of Jesus' death for sin—results in God's just judgment. The angel in charge of the waters proclaims God's righteous retribution—blood for blood (v. 6). A response comes from the altar: "Yes, Lord God Almighty, true and just are your judgments" (cp. 6:9).

The fourth bowl is poured on the sun, resulting in intensification of its heat, in contrast to the redeemed who come out of the Great Tribulation with the promise: "The sun will not beat upon them, nor any scorching heat" (7:16).

"Rid yourselves of all the offenses you have committed, and get a new heart and a new spirit. Why will you die, O house of Israel? For I take no pleasure in the death of anyone, declares the Sovereign LORD. Repent and live!" (Ezek. 18:31–32).

The earth dwellers in their rebellion are scorched, and they scream out in hatred against God. As painful as all of these judgments have been, God takes no delight in sin or death. He desires people to trust His salvation (Ezek. 18:30–32). Yet the terrible picture in this section is of people so hardened in their ways and so committed to false religions that they will not repent (or "change their thinking").

The fifth bowl is poured out on the kingdom of the beast, which is plunged into darkness, much like the ninth Egyptian plague (Exod. 10:22) and the fourth trumpet (Rev. 8:12). In Egyptian religion, Re (Ra) was the sun god. This was the primary deity whose worship was centered in the city of Heliopolis. The pharaoh was named after Re and called the son of god. Thus, the plague of darkness was a judgment on the Egyptian false religion and its leader. In a similar way, the fifth bowl judgment falls upon the king and his kingdom. Satan, who is also called "Lucifer" (Lat., "light-bearer"), is the false god behind the beast. Satan, who transforms himself into an angel of light (2 Cor. 11:14) and who blinds people so that they cannot see the light of the glorious gospel, has his kingdom shown for what it is. It is the kingdom of darkness

(Col. 1:13; cp. Rev. 8:12; 9:2; 18:23; Exod. 10:22; Isa. 8:19–22; Amos 5:18, 20; Zeph. 1:15; Matt. 25:30).

In spite of the revelation of God in the judgments and of the false god and his kingdom, the world remains in its rebellion. They blaspheme God and refuse to repent.

The sixth bowl judgment differs from the previous bowls in that it is a preparation for the final battle. The great river Euphrates was the ideal boundary of the Holy Land. Beyond it, world empires and their troops (Assyrians and Babylonians) went forth to conquer. Babylon, the fountain of rebellion against God, was there. The sixth trumpet judgment (9:13–21) also describes part of the process for the end-time world battle. In this vision, the "kings of the east" (any nation east of the Euphrates River) are led by Satan's demons. The frog was an unclean animal to the Jews, and it was also a symbol of Persian and Egyptian gods or goddesses. Thus, it was doubly unclean and an apt description for satanic spirits.

The focal assembly for the kings of the east is "Harmagedon" (Armageddon). Many (some say 200!) great battles have been fought on the plains of Megiddo, and so this is a fitting place for the final great battle. In verse 15 a call from Jesus Christ warns of His unexpected coming (cp. 3:3; Matt. 24:43; Luke 12:39; 1 Thess. 5:2; 2 Pet. 3:10), and He also pronounces a blessing on those who stay away. No one has been able to give a good explanation of the origin of the name "Harmagedon" (Mount of Megiddo) since Megiddo is a city in a great plain. The meaning of the term is the eschatological battle between Jesus Christ and Satan and his forces.

The seventh bowl is the culmination of the plagues. From God's throne and His temple one Greek word sounds (*"gegonen!"*—"it is done!"). With this, the judgment of Babylon will be accomplished. This is the pronouncement, and the details come in the next visions (chaps. 17, 18, 19). A shaking of the world kingdoms occurs with great earthquakes. John tells us that this is the most violent earthquake ever. Apocalyptic signs and sounds occur with one-hundred-pound hailstones crashing onto the earth.

- *The final series of judgments ends with the*
- *doom of Babylon and the return of Jesus the*
- *Messiah to rule.*

QUESTIONS TO GUIDE YOUR STUDY

1. Why do we have trouble understanding the justice and holiness of God in judgment?
2. How does Satan work in world governments?
3. How should Christians prepare for the Lord's coming?

Judgments in Exodus and Revelation

	PLAGUES	"SEALS"	"TRUMPETS"	"BOWLS"
Num.	Exodus 7:1–12:29	Revelation 6:1–17	Revelation 8:1–9:21	Revelation 15:1–16:16
1.	Water (7:20) becomes blood	Conquest	Vegetation judged	Loathsome sores
2.	Frogs (8:6)	World war	Seas struck	Seas to blood
3.	Gnats (8:17)	Scarcity/ famine	Inland waters struck	Inland waters to blood
4.	Flies (8:24)	Death of one-fourth	Cosmic signs	Solar flares
5.	Cattle (9:6) destroyed	Cry of martyrs	Demonic locusts	Darkness on Satan's kingdom
6.	Boils (9:10)	Cosmic signs	Angels from Euphrates	Demonic forces from the Euphrates
7.	Hail (9:23)	—	—	Great cosmic and earthly disturbances
8.	Locusts (10:13)			
9.	Darkness (10:22)			
10.	Firstborn killed (12:29)			

The Four Major Visions

The book of Revelation in the Greek text has been divided into as many as 102 segments or paragraphs. Attempts to divide the material into larger units based on phrases in Greek such as "after this I saw" (4:1; 7:1; 7:9; 15:5; 18:1; etc.) as indicating major breaks, and minor or subordinate visions, are not successful in this writer's view. However, four major visions can be isolated based on content:

1. The Glorified Christ and His Church (1:9–3:22).
2. Christ the Lamb and His Judgments (4:1–16:21).
3. The Conquering Christ (17:1–21:8).
4. Christ and His Bride in Consummation: The New Jerusalem (21:9–22:5).

THE VISION OF THE GREAT PROSTITUTE SITTING UPON THE SCARLET BEAST (17:1–6)

If this division is followed, then a major division begins with chapter 17. The angelic guide shows John a new strange vision of a great prostitute who is seated on many waters. Pictures in "ancient art show cities as their patron goddess, often enthroned on the shore of a river" (Keener, *IVP Bible Background Commentary, New Testament*, 1993, p. 805). Rome is on the water as is almost every major ancient city. So either Rome or Babylon could be in view here, either standing for the literal Rome or Babylon or as a symbol for the last great capital city. Favoring the view that Babylon is in view is Jeremiah 51:7 and 51:13: "You who live by many waters and are rich in treasures."

This prostitute has shared her vices and corruption with the world powers (cp. Jer. 51:7). John is carried into a desert (v. 3), and the woman is with the beast (Rev. 13:1; cp. Isa. 14:23; 21:1). The color shows the connection to the great red dragon (Satan). The cup in her hand is similar to a vision of Jeremiah (51:6–7) where the nations are drunk with Babylon's filth. The woman is also a "mystery" in that she is the mother of idolatrous filth and of persecutions of the righteous.

THE INTERPRETATION OF THE PROSTITUTE AND BEAST VISION (17:7–17)

John is amazed at the great personification and embodiment of evil in the woman and the beast. An interpreting angel begins to explain some of the features of the vision to John. The beast is a world empire as in Daniel 7. This world empire had a past existence but ceased to exist. However, it will come back as a manifestation of Satan ("out of the Abyss"). The whole world will be amazed at the startling recovery of this empire.

In verses 9 and 10, the beast is connected to the city of Rome which sits upon seven hills. But the angel says that the seven hills are also seven kings. "Hills" or "mountains" are often symbols for kings or kingdoms (Dan. 2:35; Jer. 51:25; Isa. 2:2). Kings and their kingdoms are often interchanged in prophetic literature. So the beast seems to be the final form of past world empires. Five world empires were past, Rome was in existence then, and a final form will arise. If this is correct, the five world empires are Egypt, Assyria, Babylon, Medo-Persia, and Greece. Rome in John's days (about A.D. 96) was the contemporary form of the beast's kingdom. A seventh kingdom will arise which will transmute into the eighth. The eighth will be Satan's masterwork with total domination of the world.

The horns are also interpreted by the angel (v. 12). They are ten kings and their kingdoms which are not yet in existence. But they will arise with the same satanic empowerment as the beast. These ten kingdoms will be united in purpose with the beast and make war against Jesus Christ, who is the Lamb. The angel assured John that the Lamb has complete sovereign power. He will be victorious and all His followers will share in that victory. The interpretation is very similar to Daniel's night vision of the Son of Man (7:13–14). Daniel also has an angel who interprets for him.

It is impossible to predict where and when these ten kingdoms (Dan. 7:24, 26) will come on the scene of world history. Most interpreters who

Angels

Angels in the Bible are seen in many roles. The angels of God carry out His will in judgments; in the protection of His people (Isa. 37:36); in the worship of God (Rev. 5:11–12); and in revelation. The interpreting angel is often found in the Bible where he makes clear or makes known God's visions (Zech. 1–6; Rev. 17:7; 21:9–15). The book of Hebrews compares and contrasts Jesus with the angels (1:1–14).

venture a guess favor the nations in a revived Rome, that is, European. But they could come from anywhere in the Mediterranean area or the Middle East.

In verses 15–18, a satanic civil war takes place. The beast and the ten horns (ten kings or kingdoms) destroy the position and power of the great prostitute. Modern history has many examples of political alliances being formed to gain power only to result in betrayal and death once the power is achieved. Both Lenin and Hitler turned on their former allies and killed them. Something similar will happen between the beast and the prostitute. Again the prostitute is identified in language taken from Jeremiah 51:13 concerning Babylon and from John's contemporary history under the Roman Empire. In verse 18 the prostitute is the city of Rome. The anti-God spirit in ancient Babylon and in first-century Rome is the woman. Her destruction is spelled out in terms taken from the book of Ezekiel (23:11–35).

- *John is shown a vision which is interpreted*
- *by an angel. A final world empire will arise*
- *and achieve total domination. Political rivals*
- *like the great prostitute will be annihilated.*

QUESTIONS TO GUIDE YOUR STUDY

1. Why is the sin of adultery used in the Bible to describe apostate religion?

2. How does the study of Daniel 7 help in the interpretation of this vision?

3. How does the study of Zechariah 1 help in the interpretation of this vision?

Christians should have confidence as they look at history. While evil seems so powerful, appearances are not reality. The Lamb is all-powerful and evil will be conquered. The evil kingdom is full of lies, hatred, and dissension. It will not stand.

THE FALL OF BABYLON THE GREAT
(18:1–8)

Chapter 18 continues the description of the judgment of the great prostitute or the great city "that rules over the kings of the earth" (17:18). Some interpreters (e.g., Walvoord) see chapter 17 as the judgment on religious Babylon and chapter 18 as the judgment on commercial Babylon. It may be that the final form of religious syncretism will achieve a temporary dominance over the final political system. But the political system will overthrow the tyranny in favor of its own deification.

Chapter 18 contains more detail on the destruction of the prostitute, while the political system meets its doom in chapter 19. Very often, Israel's enemies were political city-states. These cities were centers of idolatrous religions and vast cruelty.

In 18:2 the angel with power announces that "Babylon the great is fallen!" (KJV). This large prosperous city is doomed to be a home for the demons. The cause is its corruption and seduction in leading the world away from God. Prediction is very hazardous as to where this center of religion and economics will be located. Who can guess what city will be the final one?

Another angelic voice warns God's people to separate from the system. God will always have His people even in the worst part of the Great Tribulation. Many believers will be martyred, but some will escape and live through that period (cp. Matt. 24:22).

REACTIONS TO THE FALL OF BABYLON (18:9–24)

The major part of this section is a series of laments by the kings of the earth (9–10), the merchants (11–17), and the seafarers (17b–19). More and more the economic system of the world is being unified. Commerce, banking, and computers are tying the nations and companies together. Fewer and fewer individual companies will be left. When the great consolidation takes place, a total economic stranglehold will occur—"no one [can] buy or sell" (13:17) without the mark of the beast. When the center of this system is suddenly destroyed, everyone plugged into the system will be left in total chaos. Commerce, banking, and computers will come to a halt. Today, with weapons of mass destruction, an entire city can be destroyed in an instant.

The great tyrannies of the twentieth century (Nazi Germany, Bolshevik Russia) are examples of empires using enslaved peoples. The final tyranny will be far worse.

So it will be with Babylon. The laments are self-centered because they did not love the prostitute, but her judgment is their ruin. The list of cargo is similar to the judgment on Tyre (Ezek. 16:9–13; 27:5–24). Of particular interest is the cargo in "human beings" ("bodies and souls of men") or slaves.

A great outburst of praise takes place in heaven. Saints, apostles, and prophets join together in joy that God has judged the great prostitute and that the return of the Lord is at hand. God's justice is demonstrated in the punishment of those who persecuted God's people and filled the earth with their blood (17:6).

In a symbolic act, an angel pictures the suddenness and the complete disappearance of Babylon by throwing a huge boulder into the sea. All normal activities (18:22–23) of the great city will cease.

■ *Babylon will disappear forever in God's*
■ *righteous judgment. Economic chaos will*
■ *take place.*

QUESTIONS TO GUIDE YOUR STUDY

1. What does the angel announce in verse 2?
2. Another voice calls to God's people (v. 4). What is the command?
3. Who reacts strongly to the fall of Babylon?

A number of Hebrew words have been translated in our Bibles. Some have become so common that they are part of our normal vocabulary. *Hallelujah* is a word meaning "praise You (plur.) Jahweh." *Jahweh* is one way of writing the name of our God *YHWH*. Jewish people did not pronounce the vowels of God's name. "Yahweh" and "Jehovah" are two other ways of writing the divine name in the English language. The word *amen* occurs 126 times in the New Testament and 8 times in the book of Revelation. It is from a Hebrew word meaning "to be firm." It is used to give solemn assent to a statement or a prayer. In Revelation 19:4, it expresses assent to the praise of God. In Revelation 3:14, it is used as a title for Jesus as the faithful and true witness.

THE HALLELUJAHS IN HEAVEN OVER HIS JUDGING (19:1–5)

A great celebration takes place in heaven because God has judged the great prostitute and vindicated His servants. The singers who praise God for His righteous action include a "great multitude" which is probably the same group seen in Revelation 7:9–10. These are the redeemed from every nation. Joining them are various ranks of angelic beings—the twenty-four elders and the four living creatures.

THE MARRIAGE OF THE LAMB (19:6–10)

Marriages are almost always significant events in every culture. In the Bible, the unique relationship between man and woman in marriage is often a picture of the Lord with His people (Jer. 3:1–14; Ezek. 16:1–63; Hos. 1:1–3:5; Eph. 5:22–33). John in his Gospel begins the ministry of Jesus with His first miracle at a wedding in Cana of Galilee (John 2:1–11). In the book of Revelation, Jesus returns to earth to consummate the redemption of His people and celebrate the marriage supper. The church is the bride and is clothed with fine linen which is interpreted as "the righteous acts of the saints."

A Christian is one who is saved by grace and then is "right" in God's sight because Christ's righteousness has been credited to the believer (Eph. 2:8–9; Rom. 3:21–26; 4:6–8; 5:1). But one purpose of this salvation is that the believer will live a different kind of life. The new life is for "good works" (Eph. 2:10). So the church is adorned with beautiful deeds in the sight of her husband. The pure white garment stands in stark contrast to the luxurious purple and scarlet garments of the great prostitute (Rev. 17:1–6). Her deeds are bloody, blasphemous, and foul.

John was so moved by the vision and the interpretation that he fell at the feet of an angel to do homage to him. He is quickly rebuked. The worship of any created being or thing is forbidden. Only God is to be worshiped (19:10). In the early church there was a tendency to worship angels (Col. 2:18) or to put too high a valuation on them (cp. Heb. 1:1–2:16). Although angels have great power and privilege today, they will be judged by humans (1 Cor. 6:3) and they do not participate in the great salvation which humans enjoy. Humans are sons of God by adoption and co-heirs with Jesus Christ (Rom. 8:14–18). The fact that Jesus Christ is to be worshiped reveals His deity (Heb. 1:6; Rev. 5:13–14; Matt. 14:33; Phil. 2:9–11).

Angels are only fellow servants with humans who bear witness to Jesus. The angel also reminded John that the testimony to Jesus is the common theme of prophecy. Jesus told His disciples that the Old Testament Scriptures speak of a suffering Messiah (Isa. 53) and of His glorious reign (cp. Dan. 7:13–14).

■ *Jesus will return as the glorious King to*
■ *claim His bride. Heaven and earth rejoice at*
■ *the prospect.*

Christians should not be surprised by the return of the Lord but should be watching and waiting while working (cp. Matt. 25:1–13; 2 Thess. 3:6–9; 1 Thess. 5:4–11).

The Return of the Lord

Both the Old Testament and the New Testament speak of the coming of the Lord to finish the redemption of God's people and to judge the world in righteousness. Jesus often told His people to be ready (Matt. 24:44).

THE MESSIANIC WARRIOR COMES (19:11–16)

John sees heaven open and a rider on a white horse. This vision is different in subject and content from the rider on a white horse in 6:2. There the person begins the warfare of the Great Tribulation. Here the vision is of Jesus Christ in triumph. Kings often rode on a donkey or a mule (1 Kings 1:33; Zech. 9:9) as a sign of peace or humility. The Jewish people longed for God to come and judge the nations. As the Old Testament progressively unfolded the details of God's coming, the hope became clearer that the warrior Messiah would come. Paul in 2 Thessalonians 1:7–8 said, "The Lord Jesus" would come from Heaven "with his mighty angels in flaming fire, inflicting vengeance on those who do not know God and on those who do not obey the gospel of our Lord Jesus"(NRSV).

The Lamb of 5:5–6 and the exalted priest of 1:13 is now revealed in His role as the messianic warrior. He is the Righteous One who will rule in righteousness (cp. 16:5–7; 19:2; Ps. 96:13). Jesus is given a number of titles: "Faithful and True," "The Word of God," a Secret Name, and "King of kings and Lord of lords." His eyes penetrate into the hearts of people (1:14; 2:18) and He wears "many crowns." The beast and the dragon also had crowns (12:3; 13:1), but they are usurpers and false leaders. The true or real Sovereign is being shown. He comes with armies but not because He needs help in this holy war. All He needs to do is speak and the reign of Satan is over. The white horse is the symbol of the coming victory. The heavenly hosts come to celebrate His triumph.

The Coming of God/Lord (Old Testament)

In the Old Testament, there are many prophecies that look forward to a new day. Sometimes it is called "the day of the LORD" (Amos 5:18–20), but often there are shorter expressions such as "the day" or "in that day." The day of Yahweh is the occasion when He intervenes in human history to purify Israel, punish sin, and judge the nations. Key texts on this concept are Isaiah 2:12–22; Joel 1:15–2:2; Zephaniah 1:7–18; Zechariah 14:1–9. Man's day will be over, and the day of Yahweh's reign on earth will begin. The clearest Old Testament passage on the return of the Lord is Zechariah 14:1–3: "A day of YHWH is about to come . . . I will gather all the nations against Jerusalem to do battle . . . His feet shall stand, in that day, on the Mount of Olives" (cp. Acts 1:10–11; Rev. 1:7–8).

His robe is "dipped in blood" (19:13) because of the enemies He has slain in battle (cp. Isa. 63:1–6). "Out of his mouth comes a sharp sword" (v. 15) symbolizes the power to kill with His words (cp. Heb. 4:12). As in creation, God spoke and it took place (cp. Gen. 1:3), so Jesus could still a storm with a word (Matt. 8:26) or heal (Matt. 9:5) or forgive sins (Matt. 9:5–7). Paul wrote, "Then the lawless one will be revealed, whom the Lord Jesus will overthrow with the breath of His mouth and destroy by the splendor of his coming" (2 Thess. 2:8). Isaiah also described the victory of the Messiah over His foes in the same language (11:1–5). The phrase "You will rule them with an iron scepter" is also a messianic prediction of His victory over the rebellious nations (Ps. 2:1–9).

The figure of "treading the winepress" was a common metaphor in an agricultural society where grapes were put in a press or vat and a person trampled the grapes with his or her feet and the red grape juice flowed out. The figure was applied to the warrior Messiah who would trample His enemies under His feet like grapes:

> Who is this coming from Edom, from Bozrah,
> with his garments stained crimson? . . . .
> "Why are your garments red,
> like those of one treading the winepress? . . . .
> "I trampled them in my anger
> and trod them down in my wrath;
> their blood spattered my garments,
> and I stained all my clothing.. . . .
> I trampled the nations in my anger (Isa. 63:1–6).

It is more pleasant to think of heaven than hell; of Jesus as the Lamb of God who takes our sin than of the warrior Jesus who judges the world in righteousness. But both parts of the Revelation are biblical, and both are to be believed and taught. Humanity has a choice about how it will meet God.

THE GREAT VICTORY (19:17–21)

In this vision, only the end of the great battle between the messianic warrior—Jesus Christ—and the Antichrist and his allies is shown. The vision starts with an angel in the splendor of the sun announcing the victory. After the great battles of history, a bloody carnage fills the fields. In World War I, from 1914–1918, millions of men were slaughtered. The British lost 400,000 in one battle to gain five miles of mud! The Russians lost over 1,000,000 men in a short period on the eastern front. The grisly aftermath is a feast for the carrion eaters such as the vultures. So here, the angel calls for the vultures to gather and feast at this "supper." The "great supper of God" (v. 17) is a total contrast to the "wedding supper of the Lamb" (19:9).

The picture of the kings of the earth and their armies lying dead and unburied is horrible. For ancient people, not to have a decent burial was the final humiliation. To die was bad, but to have one's body eaten by a predator was total ignominy. The battle of Armageddon (16:16) is over and the demonic leaders are cast into the "fiery lake of burning sulfur." Their armies are quickly destroyed and the victory is total.

- *Jesus returns as the messianic warrior who*
- *defeats the Antichrist and his allies.*

QUESTIONS TO GUIDE YOUR STUDY

1. What does the heavenly "Hallelujah Chorus" rejoice over?
2. How should Christians prepare for the wedding?
3. Who are the people invited to the wedding supper?
4. What is the significance of clothing and colors in this vision?

5. If the sword coming out of the mouth of the warrior Messiah is a symbol—what is it a symbol of?

6. How does this vision of Jesus change your conception of Him?

THE QUESTION OF THE MILLENNIUM

Revelation 20:1–7 speaks of a thousand-year period of Christ's reign. Three major views have been common in the church: (1) premillennialism, (2) amillennialism, and (3) postmillennialism. The premillennial view has been popular in many evangelical churches of America in two forms: (a) historic premillennialism and (b) dispensational premillennialism. The chart below outlines the major features of each view.

Sometimes this is called *Chiliasm* from the Greek word for "thousand." But the usual term is *Millenarianism* or *Millennialism* from the Latin word for "thousand."

The premillennial view seems to have been the first interpretation of Revelation 20:1–7 in the early church. For the first three centuries it was the dominant view and was held by Papias, Irenaeus, Justin Martyr, Tertullian, Hippolytus, Methodius, Commodianus, and Lactantius. This view looks for a literal kingdom of God on earth ruled by Jesus Christ as King.

The amillennial view denies that there will be a future, literal kingdom on earth ruled by Jesus as King. Instead, Christ is now ruling in heaven and Satan's kingdom (the city of the world) will be destroyed at Christ's return. The allegorical understanding of Origen (c. 185–c. 254) and of Augustine (354–430) of Hippo became the dominant view of the church of the medieval period. Revelation 20 is interpreted as the reign of the dead believers with Christ in heaven.

The postmillennial view believes in the triumph of the gospel in this world. The millennium will come through Christian preaching and teaching. The popularization of this view came from

D. Whitby (1638–1726) and during the periods of optimism in England and America.

The pretribulation premillennial view has been very popular with evangelicals in England and America. It is based on a fairly literal interpretation of the book of Revelation as well as the Old Testament prophetic books. The major difference between it and "classic" premillennialism is the emphasis on the Tribulation and the role of the nation of Israel in the plan of God. It also has two phases in the second advent. First, the rapture occurs in which all believers are caught up to be with Christ in the heavens (1 Thess. 4:13–18). Following the rapture of the Church, the Great Tribulation of Revelation 6–19 then takes place with Christ returning to earth to rule (Rev. 19–20).

Millennial Perspectives on Revelation

POINT OF INTERPRETATION	AMILLENNIAL	HISTORICAL PREMILLENNIAL	DISPENSATIONAL PREMILLENNIAL	POSTMILLENNIAL
DESCRIPTION OF VIEW	Viewpoint that the present age of Christ's rule in the Church is the millennium; holds to one resurrection and judgment marking the end of history as we know it and the beginning of life eternal.	Viewpoint that Christ will reign on earth for a thousand years following His second coming; saints will be resurrected at the beginning of the millennium, nonbelievers at the end, followed by judgment.	Viewpoint that after the Battle of Armageddon, Christ will rule through the Jews for a literal thousand years accompanied by two resurrections and at least three judgments.	Viewpoint that Christ will return after a long period of expansion and spiritual prosperity for the Church, brought about by the preaching of the gospel; the Spirit's blessing; and the Church's work toward righteousness, justice, and peace. The period is not a literal thousand years but an extended time of spiritual prosperity.
BOOK OF REVELATION	Current history written in code to confound enemies and encourage Asian Christians; message applies to all Christians.	Immediate application to Asian Christians; applies to all Christians throughout the ages, but the visions also apply to a great future event.	"Unveiling" of theme of Christ among churches in present dispensation, also as Judge and King in dispensations to come.	Written to encourage Christians of all ages, but the visions also apply to a great future event.
SEVEN CANDLESTICKS (1:13)	Churches		Churches, plus end-time application	Churches

Millennial Perspectives on Revelation

POINT OF INTERPRETATION	AMILLENNIAL	HISTORICAL PREMILLENNIAL	DISPENSATIONAL PREMILLENNIAL	POSTMILLENNIAL
CHURCHES ADDRESSED (CHAPS. 2–3)	Specific historical situations, truths apply to churches throughout the ages; do not represent periods of church history.	Specific historical situations, truths apply to churches throughout the ages; do not represent periods of church history.	Specific historical situations and to all churches throughout the ages; shows progress of churches' spiritual state until end of church age.	Specific historical situations, truths apply to churches throughout the ages; do not necessarily represent periods of church history.
TWENTY-FOUR ELDERS (4:4, 10; 5:8, 14)	Twelve patriarchs and twelve apostles; together symbolize all the redeemed.	Company of angels who help execute God's rule (or elders represent twenty-four priestly and Levitical orders).	The rewarded church also represents twelve patriarchs and twelve apostles.	Symbolizes all the redeemed.
SEALED BOOK (5:1–9)	Scroll of history; shows God carrying out His redemptive purpose in history.	Contains prophecy of endtime events of chapters 7–22	Title deed to the world	Portrays God carrying out His redemptive purpose in history.
144,000 (7:4–8)	Redeemed on earth who will be protected against God's wrath.	Church on threshold of the Great Tribulation	Jewish converts of tribulation period who witness to Gentiles (same as 14:1).	Redeemed people of God

Millennial Perspectives on Revelation

POINT OF INTERPRETATION	AMILLENNIAL	HISTORICAL PREMILLENNIAL	DISPENSATIONAL PREMILLENNIAL	POSTMILLENNIAL
GREAT TRIBULATION (FIRST REFERENCE IN 7:4)	Persecution faced by Asian Christians of John's time; symbolic of tribulation that occurs throughout history.	Period at end time of unexplained trouble, before Christ's return; Church will go through it; begins with seventh seal (18:1) which includes trumpets 1–6 (8:2–14:20).	Period at end time of unexplained trouble referred to in 7:14 and described in chapters 11–18; lasts three and a half years, the latter half of a seven-year period between rapture and millennium.	Symbolic of tribulation that occurs throughout history.
FORTY-TWO MONTHS (11:2); 1,260 DAYS (11:3)	Indefinite duration of pagan desolation.	A symbolic number representing period of evil with reference to last days of age.	Half of seven-year tribulation period.	A symbolic number representing an indefinite time and evil influence.
WOMAN (12:1–6)	True people of God under Old and New Covenants (true Israel).	True people of God under Old and New Covenants (true Israel).	Indicates Israel, not church; key is comparison with Genesis 37:9.	True people of God under Old and New Covenants.
GREAT RED DRAGON (12:3)	All views identify as Satan.	Christ, whose work Satan seeks to destroy.		
MAN-CHILD (12:4–5)	Christ at His birth, life events, and crucifixion, whom Satan sought to kill.	Christ, whose work Satan seeks to destroy.	Christ but also the Church (head and body); caught up on throne indicates rapture of Church.	Christ at His birth, life events, and crucifixion, whom Satan sought to destroy.

Millennial Perspectives on Revelation

POINT OF INTERPRETATION	AMILLENNIAL	HISTORICAL PREMILLENNIAL	DISPENSATIONAL PREMILLENNIAL	POSTMILLENNIAL
1,260 DAYS (12:6)	Indefinite time	Symbolic number representing period of evil with special reference to last days of age.	First half of Great Tribulation; Church is raptured.	Indefinite time
SEA BEAST (13:1)	Emperor Domitian, personification of Roman Empire (same as in chap. 17)	Antichrist, here shown as embodiment of the four beasts in Daniel 7.	A new Rome, satanic federation of nations that come out of old Roman Empire.	Roman Empire
SEVEN HEADS (13:1)	Roman emperors	Great power, showing kinship with dragon.	Seven stages of Roman Empire; sixth was imperial Rome (John's day); last will be federation of nations.	Roman Emperors
TEN HORNS (13:1)	Symbolize power	Kings, represent limited crowns (ten) against Christ's many.	Ten powers that will combine to make the federation of nations of a new Rome.	Symbol of power
666 (13:18)	Imperfection, evil; personified as Domitian	Symbolic of evil, short of 777; if a personage meant, he is unknown but will be known at the proper time.	Not know, but will be known when time comes.	Symbol of evil

Millennial Perspectives on Revelation

POINT OF INTERPRETATION	AMILLENNIAL	HISTORICAL PREMILLENNIAL	DISPENSATIONAL PREMILLENNIAL	POSTMILLENNIAL
144,000 ON MOUNT ZION (14:1)	Total body of redeemed in heaven	Redeemed people of God	Redeemed Jews gathered in earthly Jerusalem during millennial kingdom.	Redeemed people of God
RIVER OF BLOOD (14:20)	Symbol of infinite punishment for the wicked	Means God's radical judgment crushes evil thoroughly.	Scene of wrath and carnage that will occur in Palestine.	Symbol of judgment on the wicked
BABYLON (WOMAN–17:5)	Historical Rome	Capital city of future Antichrist.	Apostate church of the future	Symbol of evil
SEVEN MOUNTAINS (17:9)	Pagan Rome, which was built on seven hills	Indicate power, so here means a succession of empires, last of which is end-time Babylon.	Rome, revived at end time	Pagan Rome
SEVEN HEADS (17:7) AND TEN KINGS (17:12)	Roman emperors from Augustus to Titus, excluding three brief rules	Five past godless kingdoms; sixth was Rome; seventh would arise in end time.	Five distinct forms of Roman government prior to John; sixth will be imperial Rome; seventh will be revived Roman Empire.	Roman emperors
TEN HORNS (17:7) AND TEN KINGS (17:12)	Vassal kings who ruled with Rome's permission	Symbolic of earthly powers that will be subservient to Antichrist.	Ten kingdoms arising in future out of revived Roman Empire.	Symbolic of earthly powers

Millennial Perspectives on Revelation

POINT OF INTERPRETATION	AMILLENNIAL	HISTORICAL PREMILLENNIAL	DISPENSATIONAL PREMILLENNIAL	POSTMILLENNIAL
BRIDE, WIFE (19:7)	Total of all the redeemed		The Church; does not include Old Testament saints or tribulation saints.	Total of all the redeemed
MARRIAGE SUPPER (19:9)	Climax of the age; symbolizes complete union of Christ with His people.	Union of Christ with His people at His coming.	Union of Christ with His church accompanied by Old Testament saints and tribulation saints.	Union of Christ with His people
ONE ON WHITE HORSE (19:11–16)	Vision of Christ's victory over pagan Rome; return of Christ occurs in connection with events of 20:7–10.	Second Coming of Christ		Vision of Christ's victory
BATTLE OF ARMAGEDDON (19:19–21; SEE 16:16)	Not literally at end of time but symbolizes power of God's world overcoming evil; principle applies to all ages.	Literal event of some kind at end time but not literal battle with military weapons; occurs at Christ's return at beginning of millennium.	Literal bloody battle at Armageddon (Valley of Megiddo) at end of great tribulation between kings of the East and federation of nations of new Rome; they are all defeated by blast from Christ's mouth and then millennium begins.	Symbolizes power of God's Word overcoming evil forces.

Millennial Perspectives on Revelation

POINT OF INTERPRETATION	AMILLENNIAL	HISTORICAL PREMILLENNIAL	DISPENSATIONAL PREMILLENNIAL	POSTMILLENNIAL
GREAT SUPPER (19:17)	Stands in contrast to marriage supper		Concludes series of judgments and opens way for kingdom to be established.	Stands in contrast to marriage supper.
BINDING OF SATAN (20:2)	Symbolic of Christ's resurrection victory over Satan.	Curbing of Satan's power during the millennium		Symbolic of Christ's victory over Satan.
MILLENNIUM (20:2–6)	Symbolic reference to period from Christ's first coming to His second.	A historical event, though length of one thousand years may be symbolic, after Armageddon during which Christ rules with His people.	A literal thousand-year period after the church age during which Christ rules with His people but especially through the Jews.	A lengthy period of expansion and spiritual prosperity brought about by the preaching of the gospel.
THOSE ON THRONES (20:4)	Martyrs in heaven; their presence with God is a judgment on those who killed them.	Saints and martyrs who rule with Christ in the millennium.	The redeemed ruling with Christ, appearing and disappearing on earth at will to oversee life on earth.	Saints and martyrs who rule with Christ.

Millennial Perspectives on Revelation

Point of Interpretation	Amillennial	Historical Premillennial	Dispensational Premillennial	Postmillennial
First Resurrection (20:5–6)	The spiritual presence with Christ of the redeemed that occurs after physical death.	Resurrection of saints at beginning of millennium when Christ returns.	Includes three groups: (1) those raptured with church (4:1); (2) Jewish tribulation saints during tribulation (11:11); (3) other Jewish believers at beginning of millennium (20:5–6).	The spiritual presence of the redeemed with Christ.
Second death (20:6)	Spiritual death, eternal separation from God			
New heavens and earth (21:1)	A new order; redeemed earth			
New Jerusalem (21:2–5)	God dwelling with His saints in the new age after all other end-time events.			

THE MILLENNIUM (20:1–6)

Why God has permitted sin and rebellion is a much-discussed question. The Bible is quite clear as to God's sovereignty and His power. In this vision, John sees an angel binding Satan for one thousand years and then his final destiny in the lake of fire (v. 10). One angel is all it takes—not even an archangel or Christ is needed to do the task. Satan's confinement is in the abyss so he cannot deceive the world and lead people into false worship and opposition to God. But in verse 3 a sobering note is sounded: "After that [one thousand years], he must be set free for a short time." The release of Satan to test humanity once again is revealed.

WHAT IS THE PURPOSE OF THIS 1,000-YEAR PERIOD?

1. It is the answer to prayers of Christians in every age who have prayed: "Your kingdom come, Your will be done on earth as in heaven."

2. It is the fulfillment of the many prophecies given to the nation of Israel. For example, Isaiah wrote of the days in which "the wolf will live with the lamb" (11:1–10), and when "they will beat their swords into plowshares" and "nation will not take up sword against nation" (2:1–4, cp. Jer. 31:31–34; Ezek. 36:22–28; Zech. 14:9–21; Luke 1:32–33).

3. It is the demonstration of how man should live on earth. The last Adam will overcome the failure of the first Adam.

4. It is the period for rewards for God's servants and especially the martyrs (Matt. 19:28–29; 2 Tim. 4:8; Rev. 20:4).

5. It will be a further revelation of the glories of the Messiah as people and angels come to see Him without the limitations of sinful environment.

WHAT IS THE PURPOSE OF THIS 1,000-YEAR PERIOD?

6. It will also reveal the deep-seated problem in the human heart. Man's problem is not primarily Satan or sinful environment. Evidently at the return of Christ, only believers will enter the millennium. Those still living on earth will have "normal" lives—marriages and children. So at the end of the period, there will be a sifting of humanity by Satan.

7. It will also become an interim phase into the eternal reign of God (1 Cor. 15:23–25) and preparation for the new heavens and new earth (Rev. 21:1; 2 Pet. 3:13).

At the start of the one-thousand-year period, there is the first resurrection (1 Thess. 4:14, 16; 1 Cor. 15:22–23; Dan. 7:9, 22, 27; 12:29) and the reign with Christ. John does not reveal anything about the actual conditions of the millennium. The Bible speaks very little about the conditions of the resurrection body or of heaven. The emphasis in this passage is the resurrection of the martyrs of the Tribulation period. But in other places, we know that every believer will participate in the reign of Christ (Rev. 2:26–28; 3:12, 21; 5:10) and thus in the first resurrection (cp. John 5:29; 1 Cor. 15:12; 1 Thess. 4:13). The remainder of the dead are raised to the great white throne judgment (20:11–15).

■ *Jesus, the Messiah, will take over the rule of*
■ *the earth. Satan will be bound and a golden*
■ *age of the fulfillment of the prophecies will*
■ *take place.*

THE DOOM OF SATAN (20:7–10)

In the book of Revelation, Satan is continually defeated: in 12:9 he is cast out of heaven to earth; in 20:1–3 he is cast into the pit or abyss; and now he is thrown into the lake of fire. A strange thing happens at the end of the one-thousand-year reign. Satan is released, nations are deceived, and a final assault is made against the beloved city of Jerusalem. Satan has completed his task in revealing the hidden sin of the hearts of humanity and now reaches his final doom.

The background for this vision is Ezekiel 38–39 where "Gog and Magog" attack Israel only to be destroyed by God. So here, fire falls from heaven and the hostile armies perish.

■ *Even in a perfect environment, when all*
■ *people have an opportunity to know the Lord*
■ *personally, some will use their freedom to*
■ *rebel against God.*

THE LAST JUDGMENT (20:11–15)

Because of sin, we incur guilt. Objective (in contrast to subjective "guilt feelings") guilt is the liability to be punished. The condemnation or pronouncement of guilt results in sentence or punishment. In the Bible, God is the Judge. Unless a person turns to Christ and trusts His work on the cross, he or she will be condemned (John 3:18; Rom. 8:33–34).

In Christian theology, many people have used the term *general judgment* to describe the scene in Revelation 20:11–15. Premillennials usually teach that there are at least three distinct judgments:

1. The Bêma—or judgment seat for believers for the evaluation of their stewardship (Rom. 14:10; 1 Cor. 3:12–15; 2 Cor. 5:10). The issue is rewards, not salvation.
2. The judgment of the nations (Joel 3:1–3; Isa. 2:4; Matt. 25:31–46). The issue is the treatment of the Jewish people.
3. The great white throne (Rev. 20:11–15). All unbelievers stand before God to be finally judged.

The Christian will not be condemned because Jesus bore the guilt, the sin, the punishment on the Cross (2 Cor. 5:21; Ps. 1:4–6; John 5:22–24; Heb. 9:27; 12:23).

A large part of the book of Revelation (6–19) is about God's judgment within human history. This vision is of the throne of God who is the judge of all (Heb. 12:23). God is visible and His splendor radiates holiness. "Earth and sky" pass away in His majesty. All of humanity who are unsaved stand before Him. Christians are exempt because Jesus Christ has already been judged in our place and has taken our hell.

The judgment is based on the "books." That is, it is objective. Everything that men and women have done is recorded. All of the secrets of the mind and heart are known. No one will be saved by works or deeds (Rom. 2:1–16; 3:20; 4:1–4). The "book of life" belongs to Jesus the Lamb (21:27), and all who are "overcomers" (believers in Jesus; 1 John 5:5) are promised His salvation (Rev. 3:5).

In the last judgment, the Father has delegated the authority to pronounce judgment to the Son (John 5:26–27). Jesus as the Son of Man (Dan. 7:13–14) knows the hearts of people and is the One to whom "the Ancient of Days" (Dan. 7:9, 13) has given the dominion and the kingship. The text is emphatic that all of the rest of humanity will be raised up (the believers were raised in the first resurrection before the millennium). It does not matter when or where a person died—all will be brought up for judgment (20:12–14). The Bible is clearly against any teaching of reincarnation or annihilation (cp. 14:10–11). A person dies once and then is raised.

The issue is clear and the results decisive (20:15). Without Jesus' righteousness, there is no hope.

■ *Jesus Christ as the Son of Man will judge the*
■ *unbelievers according to truth, righteous-*
■ *ness, and works. All who are not in the Book*
■ *of Life will experience the "second death."*

QUESTIONS TO GUIDE YOUR STUDY

1. How will rewards be apportioned in the millennium (cp. Matt. 19:27–30)?
2. What do you think is the most important reason for a millennium?
3. How should we live in the light of the coming kingdom (2 Pet. 3:11–13)?
4. Why can a person not be saved by works?
5. How can three judgments be distinguished?
6. What is wrong with the belief in a general judgment consisting of both saved and unsaved?

The picture or vision of the final state of the unbeliever is terrible. It is a separation from God and a lake of fire. Scientists tell us our universe is literally full of "lakes of fire" receding outward in an expanding universe. So the confinement of the lost *could* be like being placed on a star, receding from God into "outer darkness" (Matt. 25:30)—"there, people will weep and gnash their teeth" (cp. Jude 13).

THE NEW CREATION (21:1–8)

Over fifty times in this book, John is said "to see" (usually a vision) or else, an angel is explaining to him what "he saw." Now in verses 1 and 2, the last vision is seen. The remainder of the book is a description of the details of the New Jerusalem and the implications of the revelations given to John. Over seven hundred years before John, Isaiah had a vision of God creating a new heavens and a new earth. Isaiah also saw the New Jerusalem filled with joy and blessing (cp. Isa. 65:17–25; 66:22–23).

John saw "a new heaven and a new earth." Peter had previously written about the "day of God" in which the existing cosmos would be dissolved and that Christians were waiting for "a new heaven and a new earth" (2 Pet. 3:7, 12–13) in which righteousness dwells. From Peter's words, there was an order before the flood which perished. The present order will be renovated and purified by fire. The globe or earth will still exist but there will be a new order of cosmos.

John declared "there was no longer any sea." Life as we now know it is built on the "seas." If the earth were perfectly spherical, water would cover it all to a depth of one-half mile. But John is not speaking primarily about the physical state of the new cosmos. To the Hebrews, the sea was always ominous and the place where monsters lived. The "beast" of Revelation 13 comes out of the sea (13:1, cp. Job 38:3–11; Ps. 89:9–10; Isa. 57:20). What John saw was the disappearance of evil and death (cp. 20:13).

It would have seemed natural for the final state of mankind to be "heaven" or else at least a garden like the lost Eden (Gen. 2:8–3:24). It comes as a bit of a shock that the redeemed are going to be in a city on earth! John sees a New Jerusalem as coming out of heaven to earth. The city has, so often, been the place of rebellion and the center of corruption. Just to name "Babel, Erech, and Accad" (Gen. 10:10, NRSV) starts the long line of "Nineveh," "Babylon," "Tyre," "Sodom," "Gomorrah," "Damascus," "Samaria," "Rome" and the Old Jerusalem where our Lord was crucified (Rev. 11:8). The book of Revelation speaks of the final great city of "Babylon the Great" in which all the evil is concentrated into one center. Both John and Augustine (*The City of God*, A.D. 422) have written the story of two cities.

Finally, the hopes and dreams of humanity will be fulfilled in reality. There will be a real city built by God Himself (Heb. 11:10; 12:22; 13:14). The author of the book of Hebrews wrote, "For here we have no lasting city, but we are looking for the city that is to come" (13:14, NRSV). The new city is "holy" in contrast to today's cities, which are filled with crime and corruption. Old Jerusalem was defiled by the murder of Jesus; the new city has no sin or death. John gives us no physical description of the new earth, but a limited picture of the new city is revealed in 21:9–22:5. Here, he only says she is like a bride adorned for her husband. Brides are always a picture of beauty.

Mankind has always sought the ideal city or the ideal state. *Utopia* is a name for the perfect society or environment. But *utopia* means *no place* from two Greek words *ou* "no" + *topos* "place."

A "loud voice" comes from the throne (v. 3) and announces that God's purpose to be with His people is achieved. God made man to be with Him and to enjoy fellowship together. In the incarnation, the Son took on humanity so that

Alpha and Omega

Alpha and *omega* are the first and last letters of the Greek alphabet. They are used as a title of God to describe His eternity and His infinity. They are used in Revelation 1:8 and 21:6 of God the Father and also of God the Son (Christ) in 22:13. The Hebrew word for "truth" is *emeth*, whose first letter is the first letter of the Hebrew alphabet and whose last letter is the last letter of the Hebrew alphabet. Many scholars think that the Greek *alpha* and *omega* go back to this origin.

humanity is joined to the Godhead as a pledge of the future destiny of all Christians. The destiny is now reached. God, as the Good Shepherd, wipes all the tears away from His people. There is no pain, sorrow, war, disappointment, disease, or death. Since sin is finally abolished and the devil is in the lake of fire, all of the terrible misery caused by sin and rebellion is over.

Now God Himself speaks. He as the Creator who began all things by His words (Gen. 1:3) now states He is making a new creation. He is the source and origin of everything. He is also the goal and consummation of all things (cp. 2 Cor. 5:17; Rom. 11:36). As John was commissioned by Jesus to write (1:19), so also the Father commands him to write (v. 5). The content of the vision is the eternal blessedness of God's people, and it is utterly reliable so people can stake their lives upon it.

"It is done!" means that there is no doubt about God's plans. To the thirsty, God meets their needs (cp. John 4:10–14; 7:38–39). The promises are to the "overcomer" (cp. 1 John 5:5; Rev. 2:7, 11, 17, 26; 3:5, 12, 21).

Verse 8 is a contrast to the overcomers of John's churches. Excluded from the wondrous city are eight classes of people who have not overcome the world system but rather have embraced it.

THE NEW JERUSALEM (21:9–27)

John is now shown the New Jerusalem in some detail by an angel. Perhaps it is the same one who showed him the nature and destiny of the great evil city (17:1, 3). This city stands in opposition to everything about Babylon-Rome. Indeed, it is very different from ancient cities. Most cities in the ancient world were small, crowded, dirty, dark places with a temple dominating the center.

This city is huge! It is a cube shape (or possibly a pyramid) which measures 1,400 miles in width and length and height. The highest skyscrapers of today are about 1,500 feet high. The Japanese developed plans for a mile-high skyscraper. Space satellites orbit the earth 300 to 600 miles above the surface of the earth. So a city 1,400 miles high is stupendous! No more cramped and crowded little cities.

This city has a splendor from the very glory of God and the Lamb (v. 24). God Himself "lives in unapproachable light" (1 Tim. 6:16) and when Jesus revealed Himself to Paul on the Damascus road (Acts 9:3; 26:13), it was with a light brighter than the midday sun. God illumines this city so there is no darkness and no night (21:23; 22:5). Because there is no night and no crime, there is no need to close the gates of the city. The gates of the city are inscribed with the names of the twelve tribes of Israel and the foundations have the names of the twelve apostles. In the new city, the separation of Jew and Gentile, and Israel and the church, is overcome. Both peoples dwell together.

Ancient building materials were wood and stone. Cement was just beginning to be used in New Testament times. Modern buildings still use the same materials, but they also add steel and glass. These materials are used mainly because they are plentiful and relatively inexpensive. In contrast, the New Jerusalem is constructed from precious and splendid materials. A transparent gold is the paving of the streets. Immense pearls are the gates of the city. The wall is made of jasper. Foundation stones are

Ancient cities were small, crowded, dirty, and dark. Animal and human waste littered the streets. After dark, people locked their doors and bolted the city gates. Lighting was primitive.

adorned with jewels. Ancient brides on their wedding days would wear special clothing adorned with coins and all sorts of fine embroidery. This city (v. 9) as the home for the "bride of the Lamb" is glorious and extravagant.

In the center of modern American cities, stands the skyscraper. The skyscraper is often the symbol of commerce and consumerism—the god Mammon.

In the very center of ancient cities stood a temple. Over one-fifth of the area of Jerusalem was devoted to the Temple and its courts. In medieval Europe, the center of the town or city was the great church or cathedral. The new city has no temple and no sacrifice. God is the very center, and the whole city is holy. The long pilgrimage began with God meeting with Adam and Eve; then after the Fall, fellowship in prayer and sacrifice, and then God tabernacling among Israel in a tent. Then came the Temple followed by the Incarnation and the indwelling of believers. The great goal of Creation and redemption is achieved in direct communion and fellowship between God and His people. The new city will be the home for all—angels and mankind, Israel and the Church, and God Himself.

John sees an additional feature of the city as the place from which the knowledge of God is spread. God had revealed that "in the last days" (Isa. 2:2–5) the city of Jerusalem would be a center of holiness and revelation. Justice and the knowledge of God would come from the city to the nations of the earth. In similar language (Rev. 21:24–27), John sees the function of the New Jerusalem. Some interpreters see this as a flashback to the function of the millennial Jerusalem. But perhaps what is hinted at is that the revelation of God and His redemption will be spread throughout the universe. At least, Paul sees into the future when "all things in heaven and on earth" are brought "together under one head, even Christ" (Eph. 1:10). In the future,

"The manifold wisdom of God should be made known to the rulers and authorities in the heavenly realms" (Eph. 3:10).

- *The Jerusalem from God will appear like an*
- *immense diamond. It will be the place of*
- *fellowship with God Himself.*

QUESTIONS TO GUIDE YOUR STUDY

1. How does one become a citizen of this city?
2. What is the function of the buildings in the center of your city?
3. What does architecture reveal about our interests and our priorities?

JOHN IS SHOWN THE RIVER OF LIFE (22:1–5)

John Milton (1608–74) wrote two great epic poems—"Paradise Lost" and "Paradise Regained." In a way, this section of John's vision shows paradise regained, but because of Christ we have far more than just a paradise regained. We are now joined to God as a family (Rom. 8:15–17), and we have received the very righteousness of God in Jesus Christ (2 Cor. 5:21; 1 Cor. 1:30; Rom. 4:6).

"LOST"	"GAINED"
1. "Tree of Life" Genesis 2:7; 3:22, 24	"Tree of Life" Revelation 22:2
2. "Under a Curse" Genesis 3:14–19	"No More Curse" Revelation 22:3
3. "Banished" Genesis 3:23	"Access to God" Revelation 22:3–4
4. "In the Dark" (cp. Matt. 8:12; 27:45; John 3:19; Eph. 5:8)	"In the Light" Revelation 22:5 (cp. Eph. 5:8; 1 Pet. 2:9)

In a semidesert land, water is precious. Without water, death comes quickly for plants, animals, and humans. So water is used as a symbol for spiritual life (Ezek. 47:1, 12; Zech. 14:8; John 4:10, 14). In this beautiful picture, a river flows from the throne of God. Our rivers are often brackish, polluted, and discolored. This river speaks of the Holy Spirit who gives life. It flows down the center of the great street and gives life to the Tree of Life. It seems that there is only one tree, but this vision is built on Ezekiel 47:1–12 which has a bank of trees bearing fruit. Perhaps John used the one tree as a collective for all which comes from the life-giving Spirit of God. Jericho is an ancient oasis city by the Judean desert where, because of its springs, travelers enjoy beautiful fruit. This is also true in the spiritual realm (cp. Ps. 1:3; Gal. 5:22). Not only does this tree provide fruit but even its leaves provide "healing."

Children often ask, "What will we do in Heaven?" This passage gives some answers. There will be "service" or "worship" (22:3). There will be fellowship and growing in the knowledge of God. The perfected Church will have perfect service accompanied by perfect sovereignty. The rule of God extends throughout the expanding universe, and His people will rule with Him forever (Rev. 22:5).

■ *In God's presence, His people will enjoy life*
■ *to the maximum forever.*

GOD'S FINAL WORDS TO MANKIND (22:6–21): THE EPILOGUE

The Bible is a library with many kinds of literature—law, prophecy, hymns, proverbs, history, gospels, letters, and poetry. It is a library written by many different people over the course of 1,500 years—kings, statesmen, judges, law givers, musicians, historians, generals, evangelists, and teachers. In each case, God was at work in the writer's life, so that without violating their personality or literary style, His own word and message was communicated through their words.

Peter describes the process: "For prophecy never had its origin in the will of man, but men spoke from God as they were carried along by the Holy Spirit" (2 Pet. 1:21). Paul was conscious of God's authority: "What I am writing to you is the Lord's command" (1 Cor. 14:37; cp. 2 Tim. 3:16–17).

John was chosen by Jesus the Messiah to be one of the twelve disciples and apostles (Matt. 4:21–22). He was also chosen to be one of the inner three (Matt. 17:1). John was also chosen to suffer and to have a great revelation given to him (Rev. 1:1, 9, 10, 19). The revelation was of Jesus Christ and His role as judge and ruler. What remains to be said? The last section of the last book of the Bible contains warnings, applications, affirmations, and exhortations. In this final section, the speakers are varied—angel, Jesus, John, the Spirit, and the bride (the church). Sometimes the speaker cannot be identified, but this does not matter, because the whole of the book is God's Word to us.

An angel affirms that this book is a reliable revelation from God. It is intended to teach us about the future. It is not an inscrutable mystery but God's message (v. 6).

Jesus affirms His certain return (cp. 1:17). The sixth blessing of the book is given to the one who keeps or observes the instruction given in this book (v. 7).

John, for a second time, almost worships the angel who is interpreting (v. 8).

The angel warns that only God is to be worshiped. It is surprising that John twice could almost make a terrible error. Perhaps this is to warn against the satanic worship of the last days. Satan, an angel, will deceive the world (cp. 20:3; 13:2, 4).

The angel tells John not to "seal up" the vision. Ancient books were mainly scrolls and some were sealed so no one could read them (cp. Rev. 5:1, 2, 4, 5; 6:1). The book of Daniel was "sealed." "Daniel, close up and seal the words of the scroll until the time of the end" (Dan. 12:4). John's revelation is for us now! (v. 10).

Jesus for a second time in the epilogue promises to return and reward each believer. What will your "reward" be? (v. 12).

Jesus reveals His absolute deity (v. 13).

The speaker pronounces the seventh and final blessing. It comes to those who have "washed their robes" (cp. 3:4; 7:14; 1 Cor. 6:11).

Outside the city are the "unwashed"—those who reject Jesus and His sacrifice (v.15).

Jesus authenticates the words of the interpreting angel. He also reveals Himself as the fulfillment of the messianic hope. He, in His incarnation, came in the line of David (cp. Isa. 11:10; 53:2) and He fulfills the Balaam prophecy (Num. 24:17): "There shall come a Star out of Jacob" (v. 16, KJV).

The Church (the bride of Christ), moved by the Holy Spirit, cries out "Come!" As this book is read, the hearer joins in: "Come!" "Come, Lord Jesus" and to the world—"Come to Him." In spite of the sovereign plan of the God who knows the end from the beginning, yet there is a universal offer of salvation to everyone. God has no delight in the death of the wicked. "Come!" "Be earnest, and repent" declares the sovereign Lord (v. 17; 3:19).

John, knowing his authority was from God, warned against any change in this word by addition or subtraction (vv. 18–19).

Jesus for a third and final time promises His return (v. 20a).

Because the time is short and because people do not change quickly, people need to repent now. Otherwise they will be fixed in their sins and their destinies (cp. Dan. 12:10; Ezek. 3:27).

John responds—"Amen." Yes! "Come, Lord Jesus" (v. 20b).

John's benediction ends his epistle to the churches (cp. 1:4; Heb. 13:25) since he was commissioned to write to them. The benediction is also John's final word to the Church: "The grace of our Lord Jesus Christ be with you all" (v. 21, KJV).

- *God's Word through John is the promise of*
- *Jesus to come back soon and to complete His*
- *plan.*

QUESTIONS TO GUIDE YOUR STUDY

1. What is the goal of your life?
2. What are "water" and "light" symbols for?
3. Why do they make good symbols?
4. How does a person wash his or her robes (v. 14)?
5. How can a person's destiny be changed?
6. If Jesus returns today, what will your destiny be? Why?

REFERENCE SOURCES USED

The following list is a collection of the source works used for this volume. All are from Broadman & Holman's list of published reference resources. They accommodate the reader's need for more specific information and an expanded treatment of Revelation. All of these works will greatly aid in the reader's study, teaching, and presentation of Revelation. The accompanying annotations can be helpful in guiding the reader to the proper resources.

Adams, J. McKee, rev. by Joseph A. Callaway, *Biblical Backgrounds.* This work provides valuable information on the physical and geographical settings of the New Testament. Its many color maps and other features add depth and understanding.

Blair, Joe, *Introducing the New Testament*, pp. 211–218. Designed as a core text for New Testament survey courses, this volume helps the reader in understanding the content and principles of the New Testament. Its features include special maps and photos, outlines, and discussion questions.

Holman Bible Dictionary. An exhaustive, alphabetically arranged resource of Bible-related subjects. An excellent tool of definitions and other information on the people, places, things, and events of the Bible.

Holman Bible Handbook, pp. 783–804. A comprehensive treatment that offers outlines, commentary on key themes and sections, and full-color photos, illustrations, charts, and maps. Provides an accent on the broader theological teachings of the Bible.

Howard, Fred D., *1, 2, 3 John, Jude, Revelation* (Layman's Bible Book Commentary), pp. 51–150. A popular treatment of Revelation.

Lea, Thomas D., *The New Testament: Its Background and Message*, pp. 585–613. An excellent resource for background material—political, cultural, historical, and religious. Provides background information in both broad strokes on nonspecific books, including Revelation.

Robertson, A. T., *Word Pictures in the New Testament*, "General Epistles & Revelation," vol. 6, pp. 269–488. This six-volume series provides insights into the language of the Greek New Testament. Provides word studies as well as grammatical and background insights into the book of Revelation.